Status of Adivasis/Indigenous Peoples Mining Series – 2

JHARKHAND

Mining Jharkhand: An Adivasi Homeland

DISCLAIMER

Status of Adivasis/Indigenous Peoples Mining Series – 2

JHARKHAND

Mining Jharkhand: An Adivasi Homeland

Ajitha S George

Status of Adivasis/Indigenous Peoples Mining Series – 2 :
JHARKHAND

Ajitha S George

First Published, 2014

ISBN 978-93-5002-274-0

Published by
AAKAR BOOKS
28 E Pocket IV, Mayur Vihar Phase I, Delhi 110 091
Phone: 011 2279 5505 Telefax: 011 2279 5641
aakarbooks@gmail.com; www.aakarbooks.com

In association with
THE OTHER MEDIA
J 139, First Floor, Vikas Puri
New Delhi 110 018
Phones: 011 2854 3372/73, Fax: 011 4237 1129
Email: tom@theothermedia.org

Printed at
Saurabh Printers Pvt. Ltd., A 16, Sector IV, Noida

Acknowledgements

The Status of Adivasis/Indigenous Peoples (SAIP) has been an important initiative of The Other Media and All India Coordinating Forum of Adivasis/Indigenous Peoples. It began with a lot of interest and enthusiasm with a wide consultation among activists, scholars and researchers interested in Adivasis/Indigenous People's issues. However, the process seemed to have had its own pace and could not keep up with the expectation of completing the report on time. The present phase of the programme has covered, state-wise, issues of land and mining in the Adivasis/Indigenous People's areas.

This report on mining issues in the Adivasi areas of Jharkhand has been prepared by Ajitha S George. We gratefully acknowledge the efforts made by the author in preparing this report.

Members of the EC went through the report and gave their valuable comments and suggestions. We gratefully acknowledge their contribution that was available at every stage of preparation of the report. The efforts of the EC have been untiringly coordinated by C R Bijoy. The reports owe a lot to his relentless efforts to keep in the loop everyone concerned towards producing good results out of the reports. At the level of The Other Media, Ravi Hemadri, who worked as the Executive Director of the organisation through most part of the programme serves as a link between the organisation and the EC. He continued to coordinate the final editing and printing of the reports. We gratefully acknowledge the role played by both C R Bijoy and Ravi Hemadri.

We acknowledge and thank the Adivasi Academy, Tejgarh, Gujarat, and particularly Prof Ganesh Devy, for generously hosting in February, 2008, a two-day workshop of members of the EC and authors to review the draft reports. We thank the members of the Advisory Board of the SAIP, who with their participation in the first consultation and later whenever called upon, gave their inputs to the reports. Thanks are due to Shankar Gopalakrishnan who meticulously put together statistical data and selected literature for SAIP.

Finally we would like to acknowledge and thank our funders ICCO, Netherlands, and TROCAIRE, Ireland, who supported the programme right through the last five years. We are grateful to the Foundation for Ecological Security, Anand, Gujarat, and OXFAM who generously supported the printing of the first phase of reports on land. We thank all of them for being patient with this initiative.

E Deenadayalan
General Secretary

Contents

Acknowledgements 5
List of Tables 9
Acronyms and Abbreviations 11
Preface 13
Executive Summary 17
1. Introduction: A Brief History of Mining in Jharkhand 21
2. Mineral Wealth of Jharkhand 25
3. Granting of Mineral Leases and the New Policies 31
4. Land for Mining 41
5. Displacement and its Consequences on Indigenous People 59
6. Land After Mining 72
7. Current Situation of Labour in Mines 76
8. Mining and its Impact on Health 82
9. Resistance in the New Period 91
10. Conclusion 102
References 105

List of Tables

1. Mineral Wealth of Jharkhand and India 26
2. Mineral Production in Jharkhand (erstwhile Bihar) Between 1991-1992 and 1999-2000 27
3. Production of Minerals in Jharkhand in 2002-2003 (in lakh tonnes) 28
4. Mineral Production in the Country 2001-2002 (in crores of Rupees) 29
5. Area Covered by Major Mineral Leases in Jharkhand 29

Acronyms and Abbreviations

AEA	Atomic Energy Act
AP	Andhra Pradesh
BALCO	Bharat Aluminium Company Limited
BIRSA	Bindrai Institute for Research, Study and Action
BDO	Block Development Officers
BMDC	Bihar State Mineral Development Corporation
CASS	Chota Nagpur Adivasi Sewa Samiti
CBAA	Coal Bearing Areas Act
CCL	Central Coalfields Limited
CNTA or CNT Act	Chotanagpur Tenancy Act, 1908
CO	Circle Officer
CRPF	Central Reserve Police Force
CSESMP	Coal Sector Environmental Social Mitigation Project
CSRP	Coal Sector Rehabilitation Project
DC	District Commissioner
DMO	District Mining Officer
DSP	Deputy Superintendent of Police
EMTA	Eastern Mineral and Trading Agency
EPH	Environment Public Hearing
FIR	First Information Report
FFT	Fact Finding Team
GOI	Government of India
IBRD	International Bank for Reconstruction and Development

IDA	International Development Association
IMF	International Monitory Fund
JOAR	Jharkhandis Organisation Against Radiation
JOHAR	Jharkhandis Organisation for Human Rights
JPA	Jharkhand Panchayat Raj Act 2001
JSPCB	Jharkhand State Pollution Control Board
LAA	Land Acquisition Act 1894
LARR	Right to Fair Compensation and Transparency in Land Acquisition, Rehabilitation and Resettlement Act, 2013
MM & P	Mines, Minerals and People
MLA	Member of Legislative Assembly
MMRDA	Mines and Minerals (Regulation and Development) Act, 1957
MOU	Memorandum of Understandings
NGO	Non-Governmental Organisation
NTPC	National Thermal Power Coporation
PAP	Project Affected Persons
PESA	The Panchayat (Extension to Scheduled Areas) Act, 1996
PIL	Public Interest Litigation
PSEB	Punjab State Electricity Board
R & R	Resettlement and Rehabilitation
RP	Reconnaissance Permit
SAIL	Steel Authority of India Limited
SC	Scheduled Castes
SDO	Sub-Divisional Officer
SIA	Social Impact Assessment
SMDC	State Mineral Development Corporation
SP	Superintendent of Police
SPCB	State Pollution Control Board
SPTA or SPT Act	Santal Parganas Tenancy Act, 1857
ST	Scheduled Tribe
TB	Tuberculosis
UCIL	Uranium Corporation of India Limited
WHO	World Health Organisation
TISCO	The Tata Steel Limited (formerly Tata Iron and Steel Company Limited)

Preface

Eighty-eight million Adivasis and indigenous peoples live in India—approximately one-fourth of the world's total indigenous population. Historically self-sufficient, forest-based communities with independent cultural identities they have been subjected to displacement, dispossession and repression for more than a century and are now India's poorest and most marginalized communities. Since the onset of British rule, and in many cases from much earlier, Adivasis and indigenous peoples have been systematically and forcibly dispossessed of the resources of their homelands. In gross violation of democratic practice, social justice and both constitutional and legal requirements, such dispossession continues to this day. It is also the Adivasis and indigenous peoples who have paid the heaviest price for the current neo-liberal globalisation policies, with their land, resources and forests taken from them for private capital in the name of 'economic growth'.

These larger processes have been accompanied by the erosion and undermining of cultural identities, leading to a loss of cultural moorings and other markers of ethnicity. Less than half of India's Adivasi communities speak their own language. State and private efforts at 'mainstreaming' and against indigenous faiths, practices and cultural mores have had a devastating impact.

Such trends have not gone unchallenged. Despite

growing differentiation, ethnicity has emerged as a strong, consolidating force. Many have organised, often with the help of sympathetic outsiders, to fight against their oppressors and struggle for the control over land and other resources, and for local self-government as in parts of central India. There have been demands for political self-determination and autonomy of varying degrees as in Jharkhand and the northeast. The state characterises all such struggles as 'Law and Order Problems', and large parts of central India and the northeast are heavily militarised in the name of 'national security'. In other parts too state repression has been heavy and brutal.

Though these processes are well-known to many and particularly to Adivasis and indigenous peoples' movements, there continues to be a dearth of knowledge on the overall status of Adivasis and indigenous peoples in India. The struggle-based mass organizations of Adivasis and indigenous peoples in the Indian subcontinent articulated the need to work towards such a task in the late 1990s. The collective process to fulfil this task was launched in 2005.

The Status of Adivasis/Indigenous Peoples is conceptualised as a series of reports on salient themes affecting the lives of Adivasis/Indigenous Peoples. In the first instance, the series focuses on the situation of land and mining in the tribal tracts of the country. We hope that the series will be effective in not only deliberating upon similar themes of importance to the Adivasi present and future, but also help strengthening linkages amongst movements, activists, scholars and all others who are concerned with the protection of the rights of Adivasis/Indigenous Peoples in the Indian subcontinent.

This series of reports will explore the history, the laws, and the facts, and describe struggles while providing an overview of current realities. The main purpose of these reports is to expand linkages and relationships between movements, scholars, and activists so that the future of the political struggles is informed and forward looking.

Executive Summary

Jharkhand has enormous wealth of mineral resources most of which lies in areas where the Adivasis live. The first coal mine was started more than 200 years ago by the East India Company along the river Damodar, in the northeastern part of Jharkhand. The Jharkhand Government's Industrial Policy, 2001 identified mining as the most important thrust area for focused industrial development. The government is going all out to woo investors into the mining sector, by relaxing rules and making procedures easy. So far, the state government has signed Memorandum of Understandings (MOUs) with nearly 105 companies for mega investment in the state.

Jharkhand has a long history of mining. Traditional communities like Asurs and Agarias were well-versed in the art of smelting iron. Prior to the advent of industrial mining, the Adivasis of Jharkhand were a self-reliant and proud people who did not want to work under any master. For them, labour was not a commodity for sale as they did not come from a cash economy. The companies had to use various tactics to break their spirit and make them work as unskilled wage labourers in the mines.

In 1972 coal and iron ore mining and thermal projects were nationalized. But the International Monetary Fund (IMF) diktat of structural adjustment compelled the Indian state to bring in new economic and industrial policies in the 1990s, thus opening up mining to the private sector reversing the earlier public sector monopoly. As a result, a flood of mining companies, big and small, entered the state with their numbers multiplying very fast. This sudden growth and expansion of the industry is now threatening the very survival of Adivasis in many places. In keeping with the history of resistance and rebellions against the colonizers, the Adivasis of Jharkhand are challenging this expansion through militant resistance and 'janata curfews' (curfews imposed by the people) on entry of any mining personnel in their villages. This is very strong in the Greenfield areas where mining leases have been issued.

The British found it extremely difficult to contain Adivasi resistance to the appropriation of their lands by outsiders with the support of the colonial administration. In 1908 the British rulers finally gave in by promulgating a law, the Chotanagpur[1] Tenancy Act 1908, that would protect the Adivasis' lands from going into the hands of outsiders. This was followed by the Santal Parganas Tenancy Act in a similar vein. Besides the above two acts, the architects of the Constitution of India drew up a separate Fifth Schedule in the Constitution giving all Adivasis coming within the Fifth Schedule areas special protective rights on their lands, culture, livelihoods and social relations.

Ironically all these constitutional and legislative safeguards and protection have failed to stop the alienation of Adivasi lands. Numerous studies and statistics show that the Adivasis are the biggest victims of displacement for various mega projects which have contributed to the national development agenda of independent India. Of the total lands from where the Adivasis were evicted, 40% have been for mining purposes. In 1996, the Government of India passed the Panchayat (Extension to Scheduled Areas) Act (PESA). This important legislation acknowledges the rights of the

---

1. Chotanagpur is an old and pre-British historical name. Together with the Santal Parganas region they comprise the present State of Jharkhand.

Adivasis over their natural resources. The act mandates the formation of Gram Sabhas (People's Republics) in each village. The Gram Sabhas are also meant to strengthen the centuries-old traditional Adivasi administrative systems. However when the Jharkhand State Government had to promulgate the Panchayat Raj Act, i.e. the Jharkhand Panchayati Raj Act, 2001, it deleted all the clauses devolving important powers to Gram Sabhas. Numerous Adivasi activists and concerned members have since challenged the propriety of this act and the court is yet to pass any judgement. The matters are pending in the courts. Apart from this litigation, the State and its bureaucracy initially voiced their ignorance of the very act. But finally when they got to know, they are interpreting and selectively using it in favour of industry.

The impact of mining on the economic, social, cultural and traditional lives of Adivasis has been devastating. Loss of a traditional livelihood due to denial and destruction of natural resources, land alienation, loss of traditional value system and cooperation, alcoholism, violence, migration, diseases and ill-health, unemployment, scavenging for survival, environmental pollution, etc. are the naked stark reality that is Jharkhand today.

However, there is strong resistance in many areas where mining companies are coming in to start new mines and set up plants. The villagers are vociferously declaring that they are not prepared to give up their lands. In many areas, they are showing their anger and dissent by disallowing 'Public Hearings' to be held. As a result, though MOUs have been signed by the state government with various companies since 2002, none of the mega projects could start dissent so far.

1

Introduction
A Brief History of Mining in Jharkhand

Jharkhand is a state where extraction of minerals for industrial use had started early. The first mining lease was granted by the British government to the East India Company in 1774 for mining of coal in Raniganj area[2], which is in the present-day West Bengal, adjoining Jharkhand. Jharkhand had a long tradition of artisanal mining and production of iron, much before the British came to the region. Some of the tribes like Asurs and Agarias, were well-versed in the art of smelting iron. Elwin (1942:173-238), Walter Reuben (1940: 290-291), Risley (1891) and Col. Dalton write about these tribal peoples as traditional iron smelters. There are stories in Jharkhandi folklore relating Asurs to the art and science of iron-smelting. There is a story which says how the knowledge of iron smelting was taken away from the Asurs, when the Supreme God found they had become greedy and started over-production of iron.

Historians agree that the colonial rule, directly or indirectly was responsible for the destruction of most of the

2. The Jharkhand Movement had demanded the formation of a contiguous Adivasi state comprising parts of West Bengal, Bihar, Madhya Pradesh and Orissa. Though this demand was not met with, this region is still referred to as 'Greater Jharkhand' in their discourse. Raniganj and other coalmines along River Damodar fall in this region.

traditional occupations and sciences in our country, which had reached great heights during pre-British times. According to Guha and Gadgil, the decline of the indigenous iron and steel industry was closely related to the forest policy of the colonial state. The Indian Forests Act of 1874 was, in fact, an attempt by the colonial government to preserve the forests for their own use and ensure state monopoly over the forests. The Act prohibited local communities from cutting trees or even branches, or breaking twigs from the forest. This affected the lives of Adivasi communities who were dependent on the forests for most of their needs and led to a sharp decline in the population of many forest dependent communities like the Birhor tribe in Jharkhand, whose numbers fell from 2,340 in 1911 to 1,640 in 1921. The indigenous industry of producing charcoal-based iron also faced extinction as a result of the Forest Act. Elwin wrote of the Agariyas of 'Central Provinces', "that due to heavy taxes on their furnaces and diminished supplies of charcoal, the number of their operating furnaces fell drastically from 510 to 136 between 1909-1936."

In the 1800s, many private individuals and companies obtained coal mining leases from the colonial government and started mining. The coal mines were concentrated in Bengal on the banks of river Damodar. By 1891, there were 91 companies involved in mining. By 1942, there were 725 coal mines operating in the country. With independence in 1947, the mineral rights in all the areas with the exception of the permanently settled areas of Bihar and Bengal were vested in the government.

Mining for other minerals had also started by the turn of the century. Minerals like iron ore and copper were discovered in the Singhbhum region. Tatas set up their steel works at Jamshedpur in the year 1907, with active support from the colonial government. Iron ore to the steel works was supplied from their mine at Goramasahi in present-day Mayurbhanj district in Orissa. The iron ore mine at Noamundi in Singhbhum district was set up in 1937. All these were predominantly Adivasi areas. The coal belt areas were inhabited by Santali people, as also the villages which were converted into Jamshedpur town. The Ho people lived in the area around Noamundi. With industrialization, hundreds of Adivasi villages disappeared without a trace. Some villages got relocated to surrounding areas.

1.1 Converting a Self-reliant People into Wage Labourers

The Adivasis, though they were easily displaced from their lands, resisted the idea of working in the mines, as wage labour. The companies had to use various strategies to convert these self-reliant forest-dependent communities into a coolie proletariat. It is said that in Noamundi, when Tatas started their mine, none of the Adivasis wanted to work there. So, they brought labourers from Chhattisgarh and Orissa. But many of them died as they could not withstand the incessant attacks of malaria. Finally, the company realized they would have to use local people as labourers as they were more resistant to malaria. Kusum trees were abundant in this region and provided the main source of cash income for the Adivasis. The villagers in this area used to be very well-off, as they earned handsome amounts in exchange for the lac found on these trees. The lac used to find its way to China and other countries along the Eastern silk trade route. The company realized that as long as the people had their traditional means of livelihood intact, they could not make them work in the mines. So they cut the kusum trees!

People reminisce in the Jadugoda area; during British times, the *angrezi sahibs* would appear on horseback and take villagers forcibly to work in the copper mines. The villagers did not like working in the mines; the job was hazardous and labour-intensive; they would run away.

The situation has changed drastically today in a cash-based economy. Adivasis are ready to work in mines as unskilled daily wage labourers, especially in the old mining belts. They look at it as an additional source of cash income and some even prefer it over their traditional livelihood of agriculture. But the other side of the story is that there are many who have been driven to penury and destitution because of mining and displacement. People are flocking to work in the mines, from both inside and outside the state. There is a dearth of jobs in the formal mining sector. All big mine owners in Jharkhand like Tata Steel, Steel Authority of India Limited (SAIL), and Coal India have adopted the policy of cutting down on personnel and expenditure by outsourcing jobs. As a result, the number of workers in the informal sector has swelled. The total number of workers in the mining sector in Jharkhand today is difficult to find, as most of them are working in the unorganised sector. There is no proper recording of labour employment in the unorganised and informal sectors.

2

Mineral Wealth of Jharkhand

Jharkhand is endowed with huge reserves of various minerals. It accounts for 37% of the total mineral wealth of India. The state is the sole producer of coking coal, uranium and pyrite. It ranks first in the production of coal, mica, kyanite and copper. The Indian Bureau of Mines reports that Jharkhand holds the highest reserves of copper, coal and mica in the country. In iron and graphite reserves, it has the second highest position.

A Report of the Indian Bureau of Mines says that Jharkhand has the largest reserves in the country in terms of copper, coal and mica. In graphite and iron ore reserves, Jharkhand holds the second position in India. Other statistics say that Jharkhand led the states with the highest mineral production in the year 2001-2002.

The following table shows the estimated reserves of the various important minerals in both Jharkhand and the whole of India.

Table 1: Mineral Wealth of Jharkhand and India

Sl. No.	Mineral	*Estimated Reserves in Million Tonnes* India	Jharkhand	Percentage Share of India's Reserves
1.	Coal	211593.61	69128	32.00
2.	Iron Ore			
	Haemetite			
	Magnetite	100523408	37585	37.000.01
3.	Limestone	75678	511	0.67
4.	Copper Ore	441	112	25.00
5.	Bauxite	2462	70	2.80
6.	Kyanite	2.8	0.13	4.60
7.	Fire Clay	518	50	9.65
8.	Graphite	4.5	0.38	8.40
9.	Quartz and Silica	2402	148	6.10
10.	Keolin (China Clay)	1042	45.69	4.38
11.	Dolomite	4386	29	0.66
12.	Bentonite	365	0.8	0.21
13.	Talc Soapstone	213	0.3	0.14
14.	Granite	42916	8847M.Cu.M.Ts	21.00
15.	Coal Bed Methane	-	1500 B.Cu.M.T.s	-

Source: Ministry of Mines and Geology, Government of Jharkhand, 2003

Table 2 gives a list of the various minerals produced in Bihar in the two years, 1991-1992 and 1999-2000. The table shows the increase in mineral production during this ten-year period. Jharkhand region contributed to a major share of the mineral production in the erstwhile Bihar state.

Overall mineral production shot up in the 10-year period between 1991-2000, whereas the number of mines came down significantly during the same period. There was a decline in the production of some minerals, but there was a significant growth in the production of most of the minerals.

Table 2: Mineral Production in Jharkhand (erstwhile Bihar) Between 1991-1992 and 1999-2000

Mineral	*No. of Mines*	*1990-1991 Quantity (tons)*	*Value (Rs'000)*	*No. of Mines*	*1999-2000 Quantity (tons)*	*Value (Rs'000)*
Coal	181	67,297, 000	2017,80,70	170	76,904,000	4623,31,44
Bauxite	34	874,797	6,13,55	31	1,227,757	25,32,05
Copper	5	1,245,862	68,18,98	4	12,640	62,63,57
Gold		192kg	5,00,06		433 k	15,73,58
Iron Ore	34	8,352,000	83,51,96	18	11,913,000	243,12,13
Manganese	5	23,526	37,03	1	6,125	20,62
Silver		14,856 kg	10,00,30		12,147	9,19,81
Dolomite	1	116,393	1,94,70	1	262,084	15,62,02
Felspar	7	3,636	3,78	2	4,741	5,91
Fire Clay	26	35,536	22,05	10	8588	10,90
Graphite	3	7,978	12,46	5	11,260	21,96
Kaolin	20	37,887	1,39,33	16	34,622	1,78,93
Kyanite	4	21,115	2,85,24	2	5,873	39,40
Limestone	28	1,402,000	22,65,44	21	1,140,000	29,58,10
Mica	55	1,944	1,50,32	14	320	33,80
Ochre	1	376	32	1	260	25
Pyrites	1	105,518	4,22,07	1	9,539	86,43
Quartz	7	3,502	2,80	9	15,546	12,19
Quartzite	6	22,290	14,05	5	26,590	26,80
Silica Sand	2	69, 567	1,06,08	1	53,354	1,1780
Steatite	3	3,313	2,60	1	945	49
Minor Minerals			58,24,26			226,25,87
Total	335		2313,48,08	314		5256,34,30

Table 3 gives the total production of minerals in the state in 2002-2003.

Table 3: Production of Minerals in Jharkhand in 2002-2003 (in lakh tonnes)

Sl. No.	*Name of Mineral*	*Production*
1.	Coal	831.71
2.	Iron Ore	129.73
3.	Magnetite	0.03
4.	Bauxite	11.79
5.	Limestone	238.26
6.	Fire Clay	0.01
7.	Mica	26.19
8.	Soapstone	0.02
9.	Sand for Stowing	26.53
10.	Quartz/Felspar	0.31
11.	Graphite	0.12
12.	Kyanite	0.039
13.	Uranium	N.A.
14.	China Clay	1.72
15.	Copper Ore	0.94
16.	Pyroxanite	0.23
17.	Dolomite	2.57
18.	Bentonite	0.17
19.	Granite	2405 cu.m

Source: Ministry of Mines and Geology, Government of Jharkhand

Table 4 gives a state-wise distribution of the total value of minerals produced in our country in 2001-2002. Jharkhand has the highest mineral production with Rs. 4,997 crores.

Geographically, more than half of Jharkhand State falls under the Fifth Schedule Area, which denotes a significantly high population of Adivasis. A mineral map of the state would show that the major part of the mineral reserves in Jharkhand lies in the Fifth Schedule area. Furthermore, major minerals like iron ore, manganese, uranium, kyanite, and chromite are found only in the Scheduled Areas and a large share of the reserves of the other important minerals like coal, bauxite, limestone and copper is also found in the Scheduled Areas.

Table 4: Mineral Production in the Country 2001-2002 (in crores of Rupees)

State	*Total Value of Minerals Produced in 2001-2002*
India	59,509
Andhra Pradesh	4,857
Assam	3,240
Bihar	984
Chhattisgarh	3,924
Gujarat	4,722
Jharkhand	4,997
Karnataka	993
Madhya Pradesh	3,160
Maharashtra	2,732
Orissa	2,808
Rajasthan	2,278
Tamil Nadu	1,711
Uttar Pradesh	2,165
West Bengal	2,292
Off-shore	17,423
Others	1,223

Source: Indian Mineral Industry at a Glance 2001-2002, Indian Bureau of Mines, Nagpur.

Table 5 gives the area covered under leases for mining of various minerals in the state in 2002-2003. The total land area of Jharkhand is 7,971,400 hectares, out of which forests cover about 2,314,739 hectares (29%). The table shows that the total area covered under leases comes to 3% of the total land area of the state.

Table 5: Area Covered by Major Mineral Leases in Jharkhand

Sl. No.	*Name of Mineral*	*No. of Leases*	*Area Covered Under Leases*
1.	Coal	206	129567.54
2.	Copper ore	3	15857.70
3.	Bauxite	41	9012.63
4.	Limestone	44	9553.90
5.	Kyanite	5	2500.16
6.	Pyroxanite	3	43.96
7.	Dolomite	2	546.83

8.	Iron Ore (Haematite)	42	32438
9.	Magnetite	9	357.09
10.	Graphite	22	3382.16
11.	Chromite	-	-
12.	China Clay	33	3787.67
13.	Fire Clay	34	4525.38
14.	Mica	15	1318.04
15.	Soapstone	6	250.87g
16.	Sand for Stowing	23	4965.83
17.	Uranium	1	1312.62
18.	Felspar/Quartz	32	1782.12
19.	Yellow Ochre	2	40.56
20.	Red Ochre	1	55.43
	Total	**524**	**221298.49**

Source: Ministry of Mines and Geology, Government of Jharkhand

3

Granting of Mineral Leases and the New Policies

The Mines and Minerals (Regulation and Development) Act, 1957 (MMRDA) and Mines Concession Rules, 1960 form the basis of all procedures related to granting of prospecting licenses and mining leases for all minerals except coal, lignite, atomic minerals and minor minerals. An application for prospecting license or mining lease has to be made to the state government in the prescribed format along with the prescribed fee. The 1994 Amendment to the MMRDA has made it mandatory that the application is also accompanied by a mining plan duly approved by the central government. Once an application has been received by the state government, it has to take a decision on it within 9 months. In order to give approval for mining, the state government needs the prior approval of the central government.

According to MMRDA, Prospecting License/Mining lease can be given only to Indian nationals and if it is a company or association, all members must be Indian citizens. The maximum period for which a prospecting license can be given is 5 years. The maximum period for a mining lease is 30 years and minimum 20 years. A renewal can be granted for twenty years, in some cases, the lease can be extended twice. But these restrictions have been modified or taken away by the recent amendments to MMRDA. The New Mineral Policy and subsequent amendments in the respective laws have allowed Foreign Direct Investments in the mining sector too; as a result, multinational companies with foreign nationals on their Boards are being given mining leases. The maximum and total periods for a mining lease have also been increased.

The lessee is expected to follow the mining plan in their mining operations. If there are any changes in the mining plan, prior approval should be obtained from the central government. A mining plan has to be initially approved by the Controller General of the Indian Bureau of Mines. Royalty or dead rent or both have to be paid by the lessee in accordance with the rates specified in Schedule I.

The District Mining Officer of Singhbhum West district in an interview with the author said, he did not know that an already approved mining plan had to accompany an application for mining lease. He said it could be given within a year of sanctioning of the mining lease! One can imagine the level of compliance of the law if this is the level of knowledge and involvement of the bureaucrats at the district level.

3.1 New Mining Policy and its Consequences on Indigenous People

The new Economic Policy announced by the central government in 1991 heralded a radical shift in the policies and strategies followed for the previous three and a half decades in post-independent India. In 1972 when the coal mines were nationalised, the policy of the government was to bring all core mining under the public sector and keep it as state monopoly. With nationalisation, the mine workers, who were earlier exploited badly by the labour contractors and mine owners, became permanent staff and started getting regular salaries and enjoying better working conditions and status in society. The new policies started in 1991 brought forth a radical shift from the priorities hitherto outlined and adopted by the Indian state. This shift was from public sector to private sector, from state monopoly to opening up of markets and global trade, from protection and job security to forceful retrenchment and outsourcing of work. The Mines and Minerals (Regulation and Development) Act was amended in 1994 in line with the New Mineral Policy announced by the central government in 1993, to Mines and Minerals (Regulation and Development) Act thus shifting the thrust from 'Regulation' to 'Development'.

The industrial policy of the newly formed Jharkhand State in 2001 outlined mining as the thrust area for focused industrial development in the state. It reads, 'The potential growth in mining and mineral-based industries is immense. This sector has huge potential for attracting large investments to create employment and raise resources. It would be the endeavour of the state government to expedite the granting of mining leases and simplify the procedures with respect to the grant of mining leases. In addition, the state government would also provide certain relief to make mining activities easier.'

The policy reads further, 'the state government would encourage joint venture projects with the State Mineral Development Corporation (SMDC) especially in the field of mining. The private sector would be encouraged to take up mining activities in the state. Mining lease applications along with project report and all relevant documents would preferably be disposed of within a period of 60 days of the filing of such applications. Suitable steps would be taken to adopt state-of-the-art technology in mining activities. For this, the government would encourage private sector participation and would offer a package of reasonable concessions on a case to case basis. To ensure raw material linkage to mining-based and other industries, priority in granting mining leases to such industries and other such facilities shall be extended.'

The then Chief Minister of Jharkhand, Arjun Munda, in his address to the 19th World Mining Congress held in New Delhi in November 2003, said, 'Systematic and scientific development of the mineral resources in the state and establishment of mineral-based industries would usher in social and economic reform in the state as well as augment its internal resources.'

The state government expressed its readiness to amend policies and procedures as required for the development of minerals. Arjun Munda continuing his address stated that 'the state government is trying to put in place a simplified procedure for getting approval from the Government of India (GOI) under the Forest Conservation Act within a fixed time-frame. The state government is approaching GOI for getting the mineral grants within a definite time frame so as to facilitate the investors in the mineral sector.'

The Jharkhand government looks at mining development as the surest way to social and economic development of the state and trying to attract private investment into the mining sector, both domestic and multinational, by promising all infrastructural and administrative support. This goes to the extent of simplifying and expediting the procedure for granting of mineral rights and amending existing policies and rules. The state government is following in the footsteps of the central government, which has opened up the mining sector almost fully to private investment.

These words, smooth and polished as they are, hide behind them, the violence, agony and suffering that mining bestows on land and people. What about the communities who are affected and displaced by mining? Arjun Munda in his 2003 address said, 'The state government attaches equally high priority to the welfare, rehabilitation, safety and health of the affected communities besides user-friendly and economically viable restoration of mining areas.'

The Jharkhand state government signed MOUs with 66 companies till November 2007, for large-scale investment in the state. Most of these companies were planning to set up either steel plants or sponge iron plants. The list includes big players like Jindal, Mittal, Essar, Tatas and Birlas.

3.2 Amendments to Mines and Minerals (Regulation and Development) Act

The MMRDA was amended in 1994 and 1999, with a view to accelerating the flow of private capital (domestic and foreign), as also state-of-the-art technology. Subsequently, corresponding amendments were made in the Mineral Concession Rules, 1960 and Mineral Concession and Development Rules, 1988. The salient features of these amendments are as enumerated below.

Concept of Reconnaissance Permit as a stage of operation distinct from and prior to actual prospecting operations has been introduced. This would make investments and deployment of state-of-the-art technologies/collaborations more attractive. The Reconnaissance Permit (RP) holder will enjoy preferential right for grant of mining leases. The period before a mining lease can lapse, if no mining operations commenced or are discontinued, has been increased from one year to two years.

Sixteen minerals have been deleted from the First Schedule. Hence, state governments are not required to take prior approval from the central government for grant of Reconnaissance Permit, Prospecting License or Mining Lease in the case of these minerals. Now, prior approval is required only for fuel minerals, atomic minerals, asbestos, bauxite, chrome ore, copper ore, gold, iron ore, lead, manganese ore, precious stones, and zinc.

State governments have been delegated powers for approval of mining plans in respect of such category of mining as may be specified by the central government. The area restrictions of Reconnaissance Permits/Prospecting Licenses/ Mining Leases have been substantially liberalized by making such restrictions applicable state-wise, instead of the country as a whole. The state governments have been empowered to grant Reconnaissance Permit/Prospecting License/Mining Lease in any area, which is not compact or continuous in the interest of development of minerals. Previously, this power was vested with the central government only.

The period for which the Prospecting License can be granted has now been increased to three years initially and these licenses can be renewed at the discretion of the state government so that the total period does not exceed five years. The tenure of the mining lease has been increased from 20 years (minimum) to 30 years (maximum) initially, renewable for a further 20 years. The state governments have been delegated powers to renew all mining leases for the first time in case of non-fuel and non-atomic minerals without reference to the central government. However, for second and subsequent renewals, the opinion of the Indian Bureau of Mines is essential.

The state governments have been empowered to grant Reconnaissance Permit/Prospecting License/Mining Lease out of turn except for fuel minerals, atomic minerals and 10 metallic and non-metallic minerals as specified in the first Schedule of the Act. The legal provisions for curbing illegal mining have been strengthened by delegation of powers of authorization for check, search entry, etc. to the state government, incorporating provisions of confiscation apart from existing powers of seizure in respect of tools, equipment, etc. used in illegal mining.

3.3 New National Mineral Policy

The central government announced a new National Mineral Policy in 2008.[3] The Policy was approved by the cabinet on March 13, 2008 and later adopted by Parliament. This new Mineral Policy replacing the 1993 policy is supposed to usher in an era of unfettered exploration of the country's mineral resources and provide employment to over five lakh skilled and unskilled people by the end of 2011. If projections are to be believed, revenue from the sector is bound to increase at least threefold from the present Rs. 18,000-Rs. 20,000 crores, with the new Policy. Foreign Direct Investments projections say that it could be as high as $ 250 million.[4]

The new Policy seeks to ensure a seamless transition from

---

3. Available at http://mines.nic.in/writereaddata/filelinks/88753b05_NMP2008.pdf
4. *Frontline*, August 1, 2008 pp.102-107.

regional exploration to prospecting and to mining, except for reasons of national security or some other specified public purpose. It also calls for the unbundling of prospecting from mining, whereby a prospector may invest in and sell data. The Policy seeks to introduce competition and a level playing field by ensuring that the two roles of the government, namely regulator and miner, are disassociated from each other. It also seeks to promote the auction of ore bodies fully prospected at public expense by public sector companies so that the government recovers the cost of exploration and revenues are generated for the state. State governments will be allowed to give preference to a 'value adder' in case of multiple applicants. This means that public sector companies will no longer get the preference they used to enjoy before in getting mining leases.

J.P. Singh, who retired as Secretary of Mines on June 30, 2008 observed in an interview, 'The new policy makes the dispensation more transparent, allows a level playing field to all and tries to inject an atmosphere of confidence among investors by ensuring them security of tenure and an objective and autonomous grievance redressal mechanism in the form of the Mining Administrative Appellate Tribunal.'[5]

He added, 'The new Policy also aims to promote the welfare of the communities living in mining areas by introducing a sustainable development framework. Mining companies will have to spend a percentage of their profits on social infrastructure and grant stakeholder rights to the project-affected people.'

3.4 Impact on Mineral Rich Areas

The new Mining Policy which has done away with several curbs or sanctions on mining and trade of minerals has facilitated a rush of aspiring investors into the state, both big and small. The new Mineral Policy, by descheduling many of the important minerals like iron ore, has brought in many

5. Ibid., pp. 107.

private companies, who are new players, into the fray. This has resulted in competition, more corruption and insensitive looting of minerals. There is massive deforestation on the one hand and displacement of local Adivasis from their lands on the other. Both have resulted in the destruction of traditional livelihoods of people. Cash inflow into villages into a few hands has destroyed the homogeneous and egalitarian base of villages.

The region around Noamundi in Singhbhum West district is a good example to illustrate what has happened. Noamundi marks the beginning of the Bonai range, which has the largest deposits of iron ore in the country. This area is at the confluence of Keonjhar district in Orissa and Singhbhum district in Jharkhand. In the first decade of the new millennium, extensive mining started in this area due to the increased demand for iron ore from other countries like Korea, China and the lifting of legal and fiscal restrictions on exports of iron ore. As a result, businessmen from all parts of the country, and even outside, flocked to this region, looking for iron ore. A popular saying used to be, 'money is raining in Noamundi; one only has to go there and pick it up.'

Many new mines were started, both big and small. During the period, 2003-2006, nine Environmental Public Hearings were held for mining projects in Noamundi block alone. Public Hearings are normally held only when the land to be taken over is more than 25 hectares. There is no account of how many small mines were started in this region apart from the big mines. In addition, a lot of illegal mining used to take place in this region and subsequently resulting in heavy deforestation. From outside it looked like a forest, but going near one would realize that the inside was empty. Stone crushers were set up in all the adjacent villages of Noamundi namely, Maralgada, Guntijhoda, Noamundi Basti, Moudi, Bara Jamda, etc. It is estimated that in the small village of Maralgada with a population of about 300 people, there were about 25 crushers and all of them were located on agricultural land very close to residences. The iron ore mined from some of the small mines as well as illegally from the forests was taken to these crushers and broken into finer particles. And from there, the ore was sent by road to the port towns of Odisha or West Bengal for exporting to countries like China, Japan, Korea, etc.

What this gold rush had done to the lives of people in the area had to be seen to be believed. There was a near-total collapse of infrastructure in the area. The roads had been completely destroyed by the continuous heavy traffic. Buses had stopped plying on the roads; as a result, communication had become extremely difficult. The only means of transport were the passenger trains which plied twice a day on this route. The area which was once well-connected to all the neighbouring towns and cities had become a passenger's nightmare all of a sudden. Not only here, the condition of roads in the whole of Singhbhum West district had deteriorated because of the heavy traffic caused by mining-related operations. Besides, there was massive air pollution in the area as a result of the continuous transport of ores both by rail and road. On Sundays, the weekly market day in Noamundi, it was a sight to see the people struggling to find a place to walk on the roads amidst the teeming trucks. Rainy days were worse; people had to wade through rivers of slush on the roads. Trucks were everywhere, even in interior villages, plying on village roads causing many accidents too.

But this situation has changed in the last three or four years. There is a remarkable slowdown in the mineral traffic in the region due to several reasons. One is the decrease in demand for iron ore from other countries owing to the global slowdown. Second, many of the illegal mines and crushers in the area have closed down after the Supreme Court directive on illegal mining when the issue claimed public attention and scrutiny in states like Karnataka, Andhra Pradesh and Goa. The main arterial road connecting this area to Chaibasa and Jamshedpur has been rebuilt and therefore, communication within the area has improved considerably.

3.5 People Resist

Interestingly, the government's move had met with stiff resistance in Singhbhum district, which was the region targeted by most of the companies for setting up mines and plants. There was a massive rally in Chaibasa on November 10, 2005 in which villagers from all over the district assembled in large numbers with their traditional weaponry. This public meeting attended by more than 15,000 people was the largest gathering of people in the history of Chaibasa. They proclaimed that they would not give away their lands for mining or industries. Following this, in five different areas where the companies wanted to set up shop, villagers got together and told the companies to keep away from their lands. The efforts of companies like Essar in Manoharpur and Tata Steel in Tentposi and Chakradharpur to set up their plants/factories were thus thwarted by the resolve and determination shown by the villagers.

4

Land for Mining

Land is acquired for mining under the following Acts:

1. Land Acquisition Act, 1894
2. Coal Bearing Areas (Acquisition & Development) Act, 1957
3. Atomic Energy Act, 1964

These Acts lay down the procedure for acquiring land anywhere in the country. The Land Acquisition Act (LAA) being the oldest of the three, the other two have been modelled after the LAA which was passed more than a century ago, much before the start of industrialisation in our country. LAA is still used to acquire land for any 'Public Purpose'. The Coal Bearing Areas Act (CBAA) is applicable to areas where there are reserves of coal. The Atomic Energy Act (AEA) deals with the production, transmission and distribution of atomic energy and discusses the acquisition of land for mining of atomic minerals.

A major handicap with all these acts is that the forceful acquisitions of land do not consider the damage that is caused to close-knit indigenous communities whose existence is closely linked to land and forest. None of these acts provide any actual space for protest or dialogue or negotiations between the government or the companies and the affected persons. To confound matters, there is a total lack of information sharing with the people who will be displaced or affected by any project. This is true for all minerals and all companies, big and small, private sector and public sector. None of them considers it incumbent on them to inform the Project Affected Persons (PAPs using the terminology of the World Bank and CCL) at the outset about possible displacement and relocation and get them prepared for that eventuality. It also comes across very clearly from the various acts, with the possible exception of the AEA, that the government at no stage till taking actual possession is bound to publish full details of the land to be acquired and communicate the same to the landowners. So, in a state like Jharkhand where literacy rates are low and the rural population has very little access to even newspapers, in most cases the people whose lands will be acquired for mining will get to know of the acquisition only when they get the notice for taking possession.

It is the normal practice for big companies like Coal India to acquire more land than is necessary for their mining operations. The excess land gets slowly transferred to the hands of non-tribal people, most of the time illegally, where you see shops, houses and hotels coming up in no time. This is done with the knowledge and connivance of the company and the bureaucracy.

Another practice employed by Coal India is that they complete the legal procedure for acquiring land much before taking actual possession of the land. In a land document related to Rajarappa open cast mine, the notification (Serial No.1282) under Section 7 of CBAA was issued on April 3, 1964 and the Declaration under Section (9) of CBAA b (Serial No. 3998) was dated December 21, 1966. CCL took possession of part of the land; the land coming under the villages of Dhwaiya, Semrabera, Gopo, Palu, Chutkipunu, and Derhabera was not taken over by CCL till 2002. The villagers from these villages were not aware that their lands had been acquired for mining by the company. Under both CBAA and LAA, the owner is not entitled to compensation for any improvement made on the land after the first notification was issued. The compensation amount is determined on the basis of the market value prevalent in the area at the time of the first notification. That means, in this case, the amount of compensation would be determined as per the market values prevailing in 1964. But the officer at the Directorate of Mines at Ranchi denied this categorically and said compensation would be decided in accordance with the market rates prevailing at the time the land would be taken into possession.

4.1 Broad Public Purpose

The LAA enables the government to acquire land for a broad range of 'public purposes'. The procedure to arrive at what constitutes public purpose is arbitrary and no guidelines exist to regulate it. This gives unbridled power to the government to define what 'public purpose' is. Being non-justiceable, it is difficult to challenge it, even when it is apparent to the affected persons that it is against the interests of a significant segment of the public, or significantly opposed to the interests of a community of people.

Another cliché that is often invoked in all discussions on mining or other 'development projects' involving displacement of villages and communities is 'Sacrificing for the Nation'. The Adivasis who are among the weakest and poorest in our society are called upon to sacrifice their lands and livelihoods, and in the process their own lives, for the development of the nation; it is only a coincidence that in this process the rich and the powerful become richer and more powerful!

4.2 Amendment to the Land Acquisition Act

Activists and lawyers, along with affected people have been demanding modifications in the Land Acquisition Act for a long time. The Land Acquisition (Amendment) Bill, 2007, which was passed in 2009 lapsed with the dissolution of the 14th Lok Sabha[6] had taken into consideration some of the

6. See http://www.prsindia.org/billtrack/the-land-acquisition-amendment-bill-2007-109/

concerns expressed by them. With increasing conflicts that sometimes resulted in violence and deaths, the political pressure to amend the Act and also addressing the various issues including rehabilitation led to fresh thinking and debate. The Right to Fair Compensation and Transparency in Land Acquisition, Rehabilitation and Resettlement Act, 2013[7] (LARR) passed on September 27, 2013 came into force from January 1, 2014. This Act repealed the earlier law. It provides for enhanced land compensation, relief for non-titleholders and mandatory Resettlement and Rehabilitation (R & R) even extending beyond eminent domain acquisitions (Employment/5 lakhs/Annuity), land for land for SCs/STs, home/infrastructure facilities, miscellaneous benefits, etc., benefit sharing with land owners in the form of offer of developed land in urban projects and sharing of appreciated value of land transferred, option of land lease instead of acquisition, more participatory with mandatory Social Impact Assessment (SIA), public hearing, greater role of local self-government institutions, Expert Committee recommendations prior to preliminary notification, mandatory consent for land acquisition from local bodies in the Scheduled Areas, landowners for public-private (70%) and private projects (80%), time lines for compensation (3 months), monetary R & R (6 months) and infrastructure entitlements (18 months) and limitation to Urgency Clause (National Security/ emergencies or natural calamities. The state governments too have a say in finalization of compensation, limits for R & R by private companies, limits for acquisition of multi-crop land, monitoring mechanisms, etc. However, 13 existing legislations under the Fourth Schedule such as the National Highway Act, 1956, Coal Bearing Areas Acquisition and Development Act, 1957 are exempted from the application of this Act. This covers land acquisitions for mines, railways,

7. Available at http://dolr.nic.in/dolr/downloads/pdfs/Right%20to%20Fair%20Compensation%20and%20Transparency%20in%20Land%20Acquisition,%20Rehabilitation%2 0and%20Resettlement%20Act,%202013.pdf

electricity, coal bearing areas, highways, petroleum and minerals pipelines, ancient monuments and archaeological sites and remains, atomic power and union government. However, compensation and R & R are however to be extended to these Acts within one year. The Act creates National and State Monitoring Committee, LARR Authority, etc. The Gram Sabha consent in the case of acquisition in Scheduled Areas has been introduced; but Gram Sabha consent is not mandated outside the Scheduled Areas where rights under the Forest Rights Act 2006 are recognised. The implementation of this Act is yet to be known.

4.3 Protective Laws

There are two Acts in Jharkhand, called the Chotanagpur Tenancy Act, 1908 (CNTA) and Santal Parganas Tenancy Act, 1857 (SPTA) both of which had been designed and enacted to prevent tribal land from being alienated. Section 46C of CNTA states very clearly that *raiyati* land belonging to an Adivasi can only be transferred to another Adivasi living in the same police station area. Similarly, *raiyati* land belonging to a Dalit or a backward caste person can only be transferred to another Dalit or backward caste person respectively, living in the same police station area. But Section 50 of CNTA gives the state (represented by the Deputy Commissioner) the prerogative to acquire *raiyati* land, irrespective of the provisions in any other section to the contrary, on application by the landlord, for purposes specified under subsection 1. These can be for charitable, religious or educational purposes or for the purpose of manufacture or irrigation, or as building ground for any such purpose or for access to land used or acquired for any such purpose. Land can also be acquired for purposes of mining or any other purpose to which the government may be subsidiary to, or for access to land used or required for such purpose. The Deputy Commissioner has been given powers to acquire land from *raiyats* for these purposes, on behalf of the landlord, who is the state government. (Proprietary powers have been vested in the

State under the Bihar Land Reforms Act, 1950). The compensation amount will be decided in accordance with the LAA 1894.

The Santal Parganas Tenancy Act too prohibits the transfer of land from tribals to non-tribals. But Section 53 allowed the acquisition of land by the landlord or village headman for building or other purposes. It also stipulated that if the land acquired is not used for the purpose for which it was acquired, within a time span of five years, the land should revert back to the original *raiyat*. But Section 53 was declared 'ultra vires' by the Supreme Court in 1973 in the case of Budhinath Mishra and Others vs. State of Bihar and Others, on the grounds that the method and principle on the basis of which compensation would be determined was not specified in the section and therefore, it violated the right to private property of individuals. The state legislature has not yet made an amendment to the SPTA to replace this section. That makes it legally impossible for land to be acquired in Santal Parganas for any purpose. But there is some ambiguity in this matter, as some of the senior lawyers in Jharkhand are of the opinion that the above mentioned judgement of the Supreme Court itself is no longer relevant, as the right to private property has been removed from the list of Fundamental Rights.

4.4 Fifth Schedule to Protect Adivasis

The Fifth Schedule of the Constitution of India lays down special provisions for the protection of Adivasis or Scheduled Tribes, their cultures, social values and livelihoods and restricts any transfer of land from tribals to non-tribals. Out of the 24 districts of Jharkhand, 12 districts come fully under the Fifth Schedule and two other districts partially. That means more than half the area of the state falls under the Fifth Schedule.

In post-independent India, with increased thrust on industrialisation and mining, huge tracts of land have been acquired by the state for mining as well as for setting up mineral-based industries and plants, even within the Scheduled Areas. In fact, this has happened more in Scheduled Areas where Adivasi populations live, as these are also the areas endowed with abundant natural resources. Most of the mining activities take place in the areas marked as Fifth Schedule Areas, as can be seen from the mining map of Jharkhand.

But irrespective of all the protective laws and provisions in the Constitution, it is a sad fact that in independent India, more than 40% of the total number of people who have been displaced by development projects have been Adivasis and 20% are Dalits. Invariably when it comes to implementation of law, the protective laws get the backseat, the LAA or CBAA, draconic or insensitive as they are, take precedence over the CNT Act or SPT Act, which are supposed to protect the interests of the Adivasis. All the mining officers and bureaucrats whom I spoke to in Jharkhand said without any trace of doubt in their minds, when it comes to mining, it is the LAA or CBAA or AEA that takes precedence. It is a sad irony of our democracy that we have these laws and constitutional provisions put in to protect the interests of the politically, socially and economically powerless people, but the laws do not get implemented or are not even taken seriously because of that very same powerlessness.

4.5 Samata Judgement and its Implications

The landmark judgement by the Supreme Court in the case of Samata vs. Union of India, categorically states that the Government does not have the power to lease lands to non-Adivasis in the Fifth Schedule Areas. This judgement, for the first time in the judicial history of India, interpreted the provisions of the Fifth Schedule vis-à-vis mining. It interpreted the purpose of the Fifth Schedule as to prevent exploitation of the *truthful, inarticulate and innocent tribals and empower them socially, educationally, economically and politically*. The judgement further defined that even the government shall be considered a non-tribal person when it comes to the question of transfer of tribal land in Scheduled Areas.

Some of the highlights of the Samata Judgement are as follows.

a) Government lands, forest lands and tribal lands in Scheduled Areas cannot be leased out to non-tribals or private industries.
b) Government does not have the power to lease out lands in Scheduled Areas for mining operations to non-tribals as it contradicts the Fifth Schedule of the Constitution.
c) Mining activity in Scheduled Areas of Andhra Pradesh can be taken up only by the Andhra Pradesh State Mineral Development Corporation or a cooperative of tribals if they are in compliance with the Forest Conservation Act and Environmental Protection Act.
d) The Court took cognizance of the 73rd Constitutional Amendment Act and the AP Panchayati Raj (Extension to Scheduled Areas) Act by stating that the Gram Sabha shall be competent to safeguard and preserve community resources and reiterated the need to give the right of self-governance to tribals.
e) In case similar Acts in other states do not totally prohibit the granting of mining leases in Scheduled Areas, a committee of Secretaries of Forest, Industry and Social Welfare and state cabinet sub-committees should be constituted and decisions should be taken thereafter. Before granting a lease, it should be obligatory for the state government to obtain concurrence of the central government by constituting a sub-committee headed by the Prime Minister and consisting of other union ministers.

This was a landmark judgement because it questioned the very basis on which Adivasi lands had been leased out for mining all these years in post-independent India. If put into practice, this has the potential of subverting the whole structure and fabric of our society. The bureaucrats, who are the real pillars of our society, were quick enough to discern this danger! The Attorney General advised the Union government that there were two courses open to the government. One, the Supreme Court could reconsider its decision in the Samatha case if another case with a similar issue was brought before it. Two, to effect necessary amendments to the Fifth Schedule, through a simple majority in Parliament.

4.6 Efforts to Undermine the Judgement

The central government, through its Ministry of Mines (Ref:16/48/97-MVI, dated July 10, 2000) circulated a secret document among all the secretaries proposing amendments to the Fifth Schedule. The note of the Ministry of Mines proposed that an explanation be added after para 5(2) of the Fifth Schedule of the Constitution for removing prohibitions and restrictions on the transfer of land by Adivasis to non-Adivasis for undertaking any non-agricultural operations including prospecting and mining. This single sentence, if incorporated would at one stroke, completely defeat the intentions and spirit of the Fifth Schedule of the Constitution and open the floodgates for unfettered alienation of Adivasis from their land, forest and water.

In fact, the Supreme Court decision in the BALCO case was a step in this direction. The Central Ministry of Disinvestment had decided to sell 51% of the shares of BALCO, a public sector company located in the Fifth Schedule Area of Chhattisgarh to Sterlite, a private company. The sale was challenged by the Chhattisgarh government in the Chhattisgarh High Court on the basis of the Samata judgement. The case was transferred to the Supreme Court and a full bench of the Supreme Court gave its judgement on December 10, 2001. The honourable judges had, in the judgement, said that they had strong reservations on the correctness of the majority decision in the Samatha case and the said decision was not applicable in the present case because the law applicable in Madhya Pradesh was not similar or identical to the AP Scheduled Areas Land Transfer Regulation, 1959.

4.7 Panchayat (Extension to Scheduled Areas) Act, 1996

The Panchayat (Extension to Scheduled Areas) Act, 1996 (PESA) is a landmark act in so far as the various powers that have been devolved to Gram Sabhas or village assemblies, especially relating to natural resources management, are concerned. Some of these powers are merely consultative, while some are actually ownership rights, such as that over minor forest produce and minor minerals.

The Act vested Gram Sabhas with the power of controlling village markets, money lending, sanctioning of local plans and managing resources, enforcing prohibition, managing water bodies, following customary methods of dispute resolution, etc. More than half of Jharkhand falls under the Fifth Schedule Area. Therefore, this act is of great significance to Jharkhand.

PESA stipulates that Gram Sabhas should be consulted before acquisition of land in Scheduled Areas for development projects and for resettling and rehabilitating persons affected by such projects in Scheduled Areas. Though this does not give Gram Sabhas the power of decision-making, it is a major step forward from the earlier situation where the people were nowhere in the picture. The Gram Sabha is also endowed with the power to prevent alienation of land in Scheduled Areas and to take appropriate action to restore unlawfully alienated land.

4.8 Procedure to be Followed for Land Acquisition Under PESA

GOI subsequently issued an order on November 11, 1998 to further articulate Section 4(1) of PESA titled: *Procedure to be followed for Acquisition of Land Schedule V Areas.* This GOI order lays down the procedure to be followed for acquisition of land for any purpose in Fifth Schedule Areas by making it mandatory that all important and relevant information about the project is communicated to the affected persons and Gram Sabhas and consultations carried out with them before the project is started. The affected persons will be given an opportunity to raise their queries or objections. In case of consensus, the decision will be recorded. If the two parties are not able to come to an agreement, the Collector would record a synopsis with the arguments on both sides and his decision will be given in a Speaking Order. A copy of this Order, in case of disagreement, will be sent to the Secretary, Department of Rural Development, Delhi. This Order can be appealed against as is the case with any Order of the Collector.

4.9 Recommendations in PESA

Provisions 4(k) and 4(l) directly relate to mining and mining leases in Scheduled Areas. 4(k) says the recommendations of the Gram Sabha or the Panchayat at the appropriate level shall be made mandatory prior to granting of leases for mining of minor minerals in Scheduled Areas.

Provision 4(l) says the prior recommendations of the Gram Sabha or Panchayat at the appropriate level shall be made mandatory for granting of concessions for the exploitation of minor minerals for auction.

In September 2002, the Mineral Advisory Council recommended that the state governments could extend the spirit of the PESA to non-Scheduled Areas of the state in the matter of granting mineral concessions for minor minerals. The rights of people in the Scheduled Areas over minerals found on their lands is yet to be realized, so one can imagine the fate of such a recommendation.

4.10 Gram Sabha's Control Over Minor Minerals

As we have seen, in the matter of minor minerals, Gram Sabhas have been granted decision-making powers. But acts remain toothless, unless the people themselves take action to affirm what is theirs by rights. The experience of a village near Chaibasa is a case in point.

The Ministry of Mines issued a circular (No.15/41/97) to all the state governments on December 26, 1997 instructing them to make necessary amendments in their Minor Minerals Concession Rules. Following this, another circular (No.3/ B.M.L. 51/97) was issued on March 6, 1998 by the Deputy Secretary, Department of Mines, Government of Bihar to all the Divisional Commissioners, to ensure that the recommendation of the concerned Gram Sabha is obtained before granting mining leases for minor minerals or auctioning of river sand in all the districts that come under Scheduled Areas. Despite these circulars, in November 1998, the Bihar State Department of Mines and Geology issued notifications in various newspapers for the auctioning of river sand for the year 1999, without informing any of the concerned Gram Sabhas.

In Singhbhum West, this auction was slated for December 14, 1998 and tenders were invited. On December 11, 1998, the Gram Sabha of Aita, a village 4 or 5 kms, away from Chaibasa requested the Deputy Commissioner to stop the auction procedures initiated by the District Mining Officer, as it violated the provisions of PESA, by not taking recommendations from the Gram Sabhas. On December 14, 1998, the Gram Sabha once again made a representation to the DC not to go in for auction and requesting him to grant the lease for sand mining in their village area to a cooperative society formed by the villagers. But these requests were not granted; the DC obtained certificates from all the Block Development Officers (BDO) certifying that there were no objections to the auction from any of the local or traditional leadership to the auction. The auction was held as scheduled. In another village called Kakutia in Jagannathpur block, the villagers had formed a cooperative society and had asked for the lease for sand mining near their village to be given to the society. The Aita Cooperative did not get the license as it involved huge quantities of river sand. The Bihar State Mineral Development Corporation (BMDC) who was the highest bidder got the lease for the whole district. They agreed to give the Kakutia Cooperative Society the sub-lease for sand mining in Jagannathpur block, where the sand quantities were much less. The Kakutia Cooperative Society failed to make good even half the deposit money by the end of the first year due to non-cooperation from the BDO and officers from the mining department.

Devendranath Hansda, a human rights activist from Chaibasa moved the Bihar High Court (CWJC No. 1548 of 1999) on behalf of the Gram Ganraj Tadarth Samiti seeking appropriate direction from the High Court to the Deputy Commissioner (DC) and the District Mining Officer (DMO) to implement the PESA and not grant any mining lease to any person or body of persons without proper recommendations of the Gram Sabha. The Ranchi Bench of the High Court on July 8, 1999 directed the petitioner to make representations to the DC and DMO relating his grievances. The order said the respondents should decide on this matter by a Speaking Order as early as possible, preferably within a period of two months of receiving the representations. The Gram Ganraj Jilla Tadarth Samiti made several representations and reminders to the DC and the DMO as per this order, but with little effect. The auction of sand mines for the year 2000 was held on December 17, 1999 as in the previous years and the lease was granted to BMDC.

After the formation of the Jharkhand State, sand was exempted from taxation and traders from the towns started extracting truckloads of sand from the riverbeds and storing them on villagers' lands. The price of sand, before relaxation of taxes was in the range of Rs. 600-800 per truckload. But the prices have risen to Rs. 800-1200 per truck after the removal of taxes and sand has become scarce now. In the year 2002, the Gram Sabha of Aita decided to levy a nominal tax of Rs. 100 per truck. They had decided to start a village fund with the money thus collected and made elaborate plans for the use of this fund, like providing self-employment to unemployed youth, starting a school in the village, getting electricity in the village, etc. But the district administration took this as extortion and used police force to stop and threaten villagers, including *mundas* and *mankis* (traditional leadership entrusted with judicial powers in the PESA). Some of the traditional leaders were arrested on false charges, old cases were dug up and arrest warrants were issued on some of the leaders. In this way, the administration managed to subvert all attempts of the Gram Sabha taking over rights over the management of one of the important minor minerals in the area.

4.11 Jharkhand Panchayat Raj Act, 2001

The Jharkhand Panchayat Raj Act 2001 (JPA) was formulated incorporating PESA as mandated. Unfortunately, this Act has disregarded most of the vital clauses devolving powers to Gram Sabhas in the control over natural resources including land, minor forest produce and minor minerals. The JPA does not make any mention of the provision in PESA regarding consulting Gram Sabhas before acquiring land for development projects and resettling affected persons. The JPA has violated the spirit of the PESA and is surely a step backwards in the devolution of power to local communities and protecting the rights of Adivasis and other poor people of Jharkhand.

The Jharkhand Minor Minerals Concession Rules were adopted in 2004 where some new clauses have been incorporated 'at the behest of the chief minister' to ensure partnership of the tribal people of Scheduled Areas in the minor mineral sector[8]. The amendments would empower the Gram Sabhas to grant prospecting licenses and mining leases for minor mineral exploitation. Hopefully, these new Acts would enable Gram Sabhas to claim their rights over minor minerals, as incorporated in PESA.

8. According to newspaper reports such as *Hindustan Times*, November 29, 2003.

4.12 Struggle in Pachwara

What happened at Pachwara amply illustrates how the various laws work in favour of the mining companies and against the interests of the Adivasi people. Pachwara in Amrapara block of Pakur district has heavy deposits of coal. The Geological Survey of India has demarcated this into three blocks, namely, Pachwara North, Central and South blocks. The Jharkhand state government, by its letter No. 47011/1(4) 2000-CPAM dated December 26, 2001 allotted the Pachwara Central block to Panem Coal Mines, a joint venture Company formed by Punjab State Electricity Board (PSEB) and Eastern Minerals Trading Agency (EMTA) for captive mining. The GOI Notification of February 22, 2002 said that the coal that would be raised from here would be used for producing electricity by PSEB in its thermal power stations. EMTA would be responsible for mining, supplying, transporting and delivering coal to PSEB.

The proposal was for mining on 11 sq. kms. of land, covering 9 revenue villages. About 640 ha of *raiyati* land would be taken over for the purpose along with 360 ha of forest land and 100 hectares of wasteland, grazing land and river. It is estimated that Pachwara Central block will yield 289 million tonnes of coal in 44 years and bring the Jharkhand state government an annual royalty of Rs. 100 crores. Panem Coal Mines had prepared a rehabilitation package for the proposed mine according to which compensation would be paid on a pro-rata basis at Rs. 50,000 for the first acre of land, Rs. 30,000 for the next two acres, and Rs. 20,000 for subsequent acres exceeding 3 acres. These rates were much less than what was offered under Coal India's Rehabilitation Policy of 2000. It was also made clear by the company that a person accepting monetary compensation lost all claims to employment and vice versa. Only villagers who possessed the minimum eligibility qualification could receive employment in the proposed mine. So, obviously not many of the Adivasis stood a chance of getting a job in such a highly mechanised mining operation.

On November 14, 2002 the first notification was issued for acquisition of land coming under the Pachwara Central block under Section (4) of the Land Acquisition Act, 1894. The villagers, who are mostly Santal Adivasis reacted by holding Gram Sabha meetings and they sent letters of protest to the District Commissioner and Land Acquisition Officers in Pakur and Ranchi, the Commissioner of Santal Parganas in Dumka, the Chief Minister and Member of Parliament from Dumka. In their letter they drew attention to Section (4) of the Panchayat (Extension to Scheduled Areas) Act 1996 which stipulates that it is necessary to consult the concerned Gram Sabha before acquiring land for any development project or undertaking rehabilitation of persons affected by such projects in the Scheduled Area. There was no response from the state government to these letters, not even an acknowledgement of their receipt.

On the contrary, the government implicated village leaders in false cases of kidnapping, extortion and attempt to murder. The representatives of Panem Coal Mines visited Amrapara block in early 2001 and managed to get some of the local Adivasi youth to support the mine by offering them money and other incentives. Raghu Hembrom was one of those young men who was enticed by the Panem Coal Mines to take their side. The young men were given the job of convincing villagers about possible advantages due to mining and threatening them with eviction and criminal cases if they resisted. The villagers were not happy with the activities of these young men who were threatening them and wandering around on motorcycles provided by the company. When Raghu came to his village on the evening of January 7, 2003, the villagers detained him and kept him under observation in a house in the village that night. But they did not harm him in any way. Next morning, a traditional village panchayat was held and Raghu was produced before the panchayat. The panch unanimously found that Raghu had gone against the will of the whole community and he was asked to pay a fine as punishment.

After the panchayat meeting, Raghu went directly to Amrapara police station and filed FIR No. 03/03 dated January 8, 2003 under Sections 386/34 against 11 tribal leaders, including Joseph Soren, a primary school teacher. All the accused were arrested in a week's time. On April 25, 2003, all the accused were granted bail by the Additional District Magistrate, Pakur, and as they were coming out of court, the police rearrested Joseph Soren without serving any fresh warrant on him. He applied for a fresh bail on June 9, 2003 in the court of the Chief Judicial Magistrate, but he was refused bail on the grounds that he was the main instigator of the trouble and that he was taking the law into his own hands. He had to apply for bail in the High Court and await the decision for more than a year. Finally he was granted bail in April 2004. Joseph Soren had to languish in jail for more than a year on the same charges which were registered on the other 10 persons as well. A PIL was filed in the High Court of Jharkhand at Ranchi in 2003 by Binej Hembrom on behalf of the *Raj Mahal Pahar Bachao Andolan* seeking to quash the orders issued by the Union of India in the Ministry of Coal and Mine (Department of Coal) by which land to the extent of 13 sq. kms. was allotted to the Punjab State Electricity Board for captive mining. Three organizations namely, Jharkhand Justice Forum, Mines, Minerals & People and *Bharat Jan Andolan* were co-petitioners in this. The petition questioned the legal and constitutional validity of the said order in lieu of the provisions under the Fifth Schedule and the PESA. References were also made to the Supreme Court decision in the Samatha case. But the petition was rejected by the High Court in 2006 citing the principle of eminent domain and maintaining that the state had the powers to acquire any land on national interests.

The petitioners filed an appeal petition in the Supreme Court challenging this verdict. But in the meanwhile, Panem Coal Mines was using various tactics to break the movement and the spirit of the villagers. They registered 31 false criminal cases on the activists and leaders. It became extremely difficult for them even within the area as they were always under threat. Finally, some leaders of the *Rajmahal Pahar Bachao Andolan* and the *Bharat Jan Andolan* reached an out-of-court agreement with Panem Coal Mines, after which mining started in the Pachwara mines in 2007.[9] According to the agreement, the company would take land on lease from the people and pay them a nominal amount every year as rent. The company would also restore the land and give it back to the people after mining was completed. The company had also agreed to build houses for the people whose lands were taken and houses destroyed and provide jobs to the villagers. When the petition came up for hearing before the Supreme Court, the respondents' lawyer told the Court that an agreement had already been reached between the two parties and therefore the case should be closed. The Supreme Court decided to hold it in abeyance and directed the company to provide proper rehabilitation to the villagers.[10]

---

9. The other two petitioners in the original petition, Jharkhand Justice Forum and Mines, Minerals & People were not part of the negotiation process and the subsequent agreement reached.
10. Mining has continued since 2007 in Pachwara, which has destroyed the unity in the villages and created divisions among the people. There are grievances regarding rehabilitation, creation of alternate livelihoods, etc. Many violent incidents took place in the area after mining started; people feel helpless and frightened.

5

Displacement and its Consequences on Indigenous People

There has been large-scale displacement in post-independence India for mega projects, including dams, mines and industries. It was the indigenous and Adivasi people who were mostly displaced and relocated in these projects. An approximate estimate shows that more than 40% of all the people who have been displaced by development projects during the period 1951-1990, and 50% today are Adivasis. This is in a country where the tribals form only 8.2% of the total population. 20% of the displaced persons are Dalits and a substantial number of the rest belong to the assetless poor.

Displacement has enormous economic, social and cultural impacts on the lives of people who are displaced. As seen earlier, most of the displacement happens in indigenous areas, as these are also the areas blessed with abundant natural resources. Even today, the indigenous people in Jharkhand depend partly on cultivation and partly on food gathering still depending on forests for many of their food as well as cash needs. They engage in subsistence agriculture and not commercial agriculture. In every village there are people involved in supplementary activities such as blacksmiths, potters, cowherds, weavers, etc. They do not own much land but are dependent on the other farmers for their livelihood.

Displacement has far-reaching consequences on the lives

of closely-knit communities like Adivasis and Dalits, whose lives are very much linked to the existence of the community. Displacement disintegrates the village community. The close-knit village communities with their common culture, traditions, values and kinship bonds, get scattered in the process of relocation, which leads to destruction and distortion of their whole value system and culture. Along with the houses and fields, the sacred groves of the village which are the abodes of the spirits who protect the village also get destroyed or relocated. This is indeed a very traumatic experience for the people; the spiritual base of their lives is wrecked. In the process, they lose not only their sense of self-esteem and self-worth, but also their very bearings which define their identity as a people.

Normally when opening a large mine, large tracts of land have to be acquired, displacing several villages and denuding thousands of acres of forest. There is forced displacement from the proposed mine site even when the villagers do not want to be displaced and resist displacement. People who lose their lands and livelihoods are supposed to be compensated at the prevalent market rates for land in that area. But this rate is fixed by the government and companies. Most of the time, it is found that the rate is much lower than the prevalent market rates.

5.1 Livelihoods Destroyed

There are people who are directly displaced by mines and many who are indirectly displaced. The people whose lands are acquired, either forcibly or willingly are the directly affected people. Most of these are small farmers, fully dependent on agriculture for their living. There are others who are also dependent on these lands for livelihood and survival, but who are not the owners of the land. Coal India's Rehabilitation Policy acknowledges the existence of people who are dependent on land for livelihoods other than cultivators, like landless labourers, sharecroppers, land lessees, tenants and tribals dependent on forest produce and enters them in the category of Project-Affected Peoples. This acknowledgement itself is a good beginning even though pastoral communities and artisans have not been included in this list. But it is a very difficult process to verify how many such people will be affected by a project and to find proper methods of compensating their loss.

Coal India in its Resettlement & Rehabilitation Policy of 2000 reluctantly admits thus: 'Coal India recognises that the acquisition of land in populated areas for mining purposes greatly affects the lives and livelihoods of the people.' But this is limited only to paper. The losses that are incurred by communities displaced by these projects are at different levels—economic, social, cultural and psychological. But it is only the economic loss that is normally addressed and tried to be compensated. The policy planners are not aware of the tribal way of life most of the time, and therefore do not understand the implications that displacement has on the lives of the affected people at various levels.

Most of the Adivasi communities in this area are engaged in sustenance agriculture; they produce just enough for their needs. They are not used to a cash-based economy, and therefore not able to handle the cash that they receive in compensation for their land. Besides, the compensation is normally given for individual losses and not for the loss of common property resources such as grazing lands (which are waste lands in government parlance), streams, rivers, village forests, etc. Displacement and relocation also destroy the common spaces in a village where the community used to come together, both ceremonially and casually, like the dancing grounds, places of worship, wells or bathing places.

5.2 Economic Programmes for Rehabilitation

Coal India's R&R policy 'underscores that they have a responsibility towards the landless, whose livelihood is often taken away' and includes landless labourers, sharecroppers, land lessees, tenants and tribals dependent on forest produce into the ambit of Project-Affected Persons (PAPs). Their

Rehabilitation policy includes plans to assist them in establishing non-farm self-employment through the provision of infrastructure, petty contracts or formation of cooperatives. In East Parej Open Cast Mine, the *Turis* (basket weavers), *Agarias* (blacksmiths) and *Maharas* (midwives) were the important landless communities involved in traditional occupations, and were displaced. To provide non-farm self-employment to them, the displaced families were given pigs and goats for rearing. But these pigs and goats disappeared before very long; either they had died, or were stolen or eaten up. Women from these communities were given training in making *durries* (a type of rug). Many of the women learnt these skills with great interest; but since there was no adequate follow-up or market support, the programme failed miserably. An NGO from Ranchi was given the contract for producing and supplying cane baskets for use in the mines through the *Turis*, who are traditional basket weavers. This programme continued very well initially as this was a job the *Turis* were good at and there was a good demand for these baskets in the mines. But, after a few months, CCL started making complaints about the quality of the baskets and the contract was eventually given to another supplier. Rumour has it that some CCL officers had struck a deal with the other supplier!

At present, the only jobs that are available to these displaced people are loading coal into the trucks at the coal dump. For that job too, there are many candidates; so a person will have to wait for days for his/her turn to come up. Some of them are doing their traditional jobs, but many have disappeared. There is no place for these traditional artisans in the new economic system.

5.3 Women: How They are Affected by Displacement

In the agricultural economy, women and men work together to produce food for the family. In fact, women do the major share of the agricultural work; they also collect various forest produce from the forest, which brings in cash income to the family. This gives them great respect and independence in their societies; in other words, a higher social status. Women also enjoy an important role in decision-making within the family and in the community. But in a non-agricultural economy, they get pushed from the role of producers and providers to that of beneficiaries. This definitely has a bearing on lowering of women's social status.

In the compensation and rehabilitation package, women find very little place for themselves. Women's contributions to the economy, community and family are not recognized. Men get jobs as heads of households, which itself is a concept alien to the Adivasi perception. A very small percentage of women get jobs in the companies, either as widows or unmarried daughters. In Parej where 595 families were displaced, 25 jobs were given to PAPs, out of which only one woman got a job.

The incidence of violence on women is high in mining areas. Cases of rape, murder and molestation are reported frequently. There are people from different ethnic and cultural streams living and working in mining areas; the relative independence and social freedom enjoyed by Adivasi girls is construed as promiscuity and taken advantage of by non-Adivasi men coming from 'mainstream' societies. Many outsiders enter into sexual liaisons with local women, which they continue for some time, even years, and finally go away leaving these women, often with children. There are many such single mothers who have left their villages and live in shanty towns in the mining areas.

Mining, displacement and migration all lead to a break-down in the traditional values and assimilation of a new value system. As a result of this, violence against women within the family and community increases. Women are increasingly relegated to a secondary position in society as well as homes and assume a victim status. Domestic violence increases in mining areas. In traditional Adivasi village communities, incidence of violence against women, including domestic violence, is rare. The communitarian structure of the village itself is a deterrent to domestic violence in Adivasi communities. Displacement and relocation invariably destroys that structure and gives rise to increased violence against women both in the homes and outside.

The workload on women is also seen to increase with displacement and relocation. In Parej area, the underground water has receded by several feet, which is a common occurrence in coal mining areas. Drinking water has become scarce; water for bathing and washing has also moved further away from the village. The common wells in the area have been destroyed by mining. The use of polluted water for drinking and other uses give rise to many illnesses, including gastro-intestinal infections and skin diseases.

5.4 Rise in Alcoholism

There is a direct co-relation between alcoholism and mining. In mining areas, there is a very visible increase in the incidence of alcoholism among the indigenous communities. One of the reasons could be the increased inflow of cash into the area and the coming in of a cash-based economy. Secondly, mining brings in an abrupt change in their lives and livelihood patterns, which they are not able to understand or assimilate. From people who had a direct everyday living relationship with nature, they get into the role of destroyers of nature. In mining towns, one can see men, both young and old, sitting around and drinking or playing dice. They seem to have nothing to do, idling away their time. Some of them are unemployed, semi-educated youth, often sons of company employees, who have no hopes of getting into the workforce. Some of them are former mining company employees, who did not attend work and slowly got thrown out from the workforce. Alcoholism has also contributed greatly to a decrease in life expectancy, particularly of men from Adivasi communities.

The increase in alcoholism has a direct impact on violence against women. Mining towns have an essentially macho culture. The Adivasi people who have had a more egalitarian relationship among the sexes, start developing a different view on women's position in society and in homes. Women also get used to this new secondary position and accept their roles. The Adivasi communities look up to the other mainstream cultures as the more advanced and superior cultures, and therefore, to be followed strictly if they wanted to advance in life.

5.5 Increase in Violence Against Women

There is a huge increase in domestic violence among Adivasis living in the shanty towns of mining areas. Women are forced into the role of breadwinners; they have to go out and work and then come back and suffer violence at the hands of the men in the families, husbands, brothers, sons or fathers, who need money for their drinks. This is a common happening in all industrialized areas, not just mining areas. Incest is considered a grave crime among Adivasis, which would merit severe punishment. But incidents of incest are reported from mining areas, which seem to be on the increase. Rapes are becoming common now within the Adivasi communities themselves. Earlier rapes were unheard of in Adivasi communities. Adivasi boys luring girls from their own communities into sexual relationships and then deserting them are also becoming a common occurrence.

Women's health is one of the biggest casualties in this whole process. The majority of women are anaemic. Statistics show that more than 70% women are anaemic in Jharkhand. Maternal deaths are quite high. Incidence of gynaecological problems like uterine and vaginal infections is very high. All these indicate the low nutritional status of women as also other factors such as lack of clean water, non-availability of health facilities and so on. Malnutrition among children is also very common and it leads to stunted development. Tuberculosis is becoming a graver health menace, both in villages and towns, taking away many lives. With the fall in their nutritional status, people are becoming more and more susceptible to these infections. Malaria is another killer disease which claims many lives every year in villages.

5.6 Case Study of Parej

Parej is a village situated to the east of the North Karanpura valley and just south of the Konar watershed on the western boundary of the West Bokaro Coalfields. It comes under Mandu block of Hazaribagh district. Tata Steel has their captive collieries very close to Parej. In fact, one of the *tolas* of Parej had partially been acquired by Tata Steel some years ago for their coal mine.

Central Coalfields Ltd. (CCL) started acquisition proceedings in this area in 1983, when they issued the first Notification under Section (4) of CBAA. East Parej Open Cast Coal Mine is one of the 25 mines supported by the World Bank under the Coal Sector Environmental Social Mitigation Project (CSESMP) of Coal India. Mining started here in 1993 though the World Bank project was initiated only in 1997. Two villages, East Parej and Duru Kasmar, had to be completely displaced for the project which involved 227 families.

CSESMP was originally conceived as part of the Coal Sector Rehabilitation project whose aim was to support India's reform and expansion of the coal sector. In 1993, the GOI formally requested assistance from the International Bank for Reconstruction and Development (IBRD) for the investment components of the project and from the International Development Association (IDA) for the environmental and social mitigation measures. Subsequently in November 1995, the project was divided into an environmental and social component, the CSESMP and an investment component, Coal Sector Rehabilitation Project (CSRP). The CSESMP was designed to assist Coal India's efforts to mitigate the environmental and social impacts of the mining expansion to be undertaken in 25 mines under the proposed CSRP. In May 1996, the World Bank informed that the CSESMP and CSRP would be linked by cross-conditionality. In the same month, the IDA granted a credit of US$ 63 million to finance the CSESMP. In September 2007, an IBRD loan of US$ 530 million and an IDA credit of US$ 2 million were approved for financing CSRP. Owing to implementation difficulties, this loan was cancelled in July 2000. Coal India however decided to continue with the mitigation programmes started under CSESMP. On April 20, 2001 it requested and the Bank agreed to extend the closing date for CSESMP by one more year to June 30, 2002.

5.7 Turis Resist Forceful Displacement

The first *tola* that had to be relocated under East Parej OC mine was that of *Turis*, the traditional basket makers, classified by the government as Scheduled Castes. The *Turis* were earlier living in Sonaghuttu, one of the *tolas* of Parej. About 30 years ago, they were displaced from there by Tata Steel. Then they settled down in *Turi tola*, another part of Parej village. The *Turis* told CCL that they would move out of Parej only after the rehabilitation site at Pindra was fully ready. The management wanted them to move out desperately because production would come to a halt. They used every possible tactic to force the *Turis* out. Mining was being done close to the houses in *Turi tola*, so close that houses would shake during blasting operations and huge cracks appeared in the houses.

Civil and criminal cases were filed on the villagers to intimidate them. Four men from the village, Rameshwar Turi, Bhola Turi, Suresh Turi and Vishweshwar Turi, were implicated in a false criminal case and arrested. The charge against them was that they tried to kill a crane driver, Chaito Mahato, working with CCL. What had happened in reality was that on October 24, 1996, CCL had done such a strong blasting that houses began to shake. The infuriated villagers came out with sticks ready to beat up the CCL workers. On seeing them, Chaito Mahato got frightened and fell from the crane and suffered minor injuries. CCL used this as an opportunity to harass the villagers. They made Chaito file a police complaint against these four men. Rameshwar Turi, one of the four, was a worker with Tata Steel and was on duty when the incident happened. As soon as the complaint was lodged, he was arrested from his workplace.

CCL had also filed a civil suit for the eviction of the villagers of *Turi tola*, saying that they were squatters on CCL land. This case went on for nearly two years at the district court, and finally, a compromise was reached between the two parties on the advice of the judge. The compromise formula included withdrawal of criminal charges against the four persons, providing plots of land with ownership titles at the rehabilitation site of their choice, Prem Nagar, and providing facilities like drinking water, school, community centre at the rehabilitation site. CCL agreed to provide jobs to Rameshwar Turi against a land owning of 2.08 acres and Pano Devi, whose husband had died in jail. He was arrested in connection with a criminal case as part of harassing and demoralizing the people. The *Turis* vacated their houses in December 1998 as per the agreement and moved to CCL staff quarters in the CCL colony. It was supposed to be a temporary arrangement till their houses were ready at Prem Nagar in six months' time. But they were still staying in the CCL quarters in June 2003 when I visited the area.

5.8 World Bank Violates its Own Policies

Chotanagpur Adivasi Sewa Samiti (CASS), a local people's organization working near Parej area, had often brought to the World Bank's notice that the targets or standards set by the World Bank for the CSESMP were not being met by CCL, the enforcing agency. This was in fact the most supervised project under CSESMP. Since August 1996, Bank officials had carried out 23 supervisory missions of which 21 included visits to East Parej. Each tour would witness a stern letter being sent out to Coal India about the slow progress in dealing with the woes of the Project Affected Persons. In 2000, the Indian government took the face saving step of requesting the Bank to cancel the future instalments of the $ 530 million loan of which only half had been given. The Bank quickly assented to this.

In June 2001, the villagers of Parej, through CASS activists, requested for an Inspection from the World Bank, fed up with the indifference and apathy to their problems by the Bank and CCL. After conducting investigations, the Inspection Panel submitted their report on November 25, 2002 in which they found the Bank guilty of violating their own policies on 31 grounds and further 10 issues of serious concern. These included: Inadequate compensation for land and for houses, resettlement sites lacking basic facilities like potable water, schools, availability of casual labour opportunities, title to house plots not made available to PAPs, inadequate compensation for PAPs' traditional land rights, no compensation for loss of access to forest produce, failure to restore incomes, failure to provide land for land, failure to provide subsistence allowance during transition period, non-functioning of the Public Information Centre, failure to disclose important information to PAPs, lack of consultations with local villagers and NGOs, among others.

5.9 Bank's Response to the Inspection Panel Report

The Bank responded to the Report only on July 25, 2003 even though they were 'advised' to give a reply within six weeks of the publication of the report. In its response, the Management discussed the issues ad constraints, which were encountered during the implementation of the CSESMP and observed that while all these problems could not be solved, some progress had been made. It also noted that in its view, the World Bank had complied and intended to comply with the relevant policies and procedures related to the design and implementation of the CSESMP and provided the panel with written evidence in this regard. The Bank Management refused to take any action on critical issues like size of plots, land compensation, land for land, cultural property and so on, except making recommendations for stepping up supervision!

The Bank also said, 'since some implementation issues such as payment of subsistence allowance and settlement of claims of PAPs cultivating land under customary tenure are outstanding, management intends to continue supervising the CSESMP till all outstanding issues have been resolved. The Management also proposes to report on all outstanding issues to the Board of Executive Directors by July 31, 2004.' (Page 10, Article 37, Management Response)

Though the sustained and persistent struggle of the people of Parej forced an international institution like the World Bank to reconsider some of its policies and practices, or at least acknowledge some omissions in their practices, it also comes across very clearly how ineffective these accounting mechanisms are, looking at the Bank Management's lackadaisical response to the serious charges made by the Inspection Panel.

5.10 The Rehabilitation and Resettlement Bill 2007

For the first time in India a legislation was drafted for Rehabilitation and Resettlement of people displaced by development projects and therefore, a welcome step. It has been a constant demand of activists, lawyers and people affected by mega projects around the country for more than three decades to enact a fair, just and inclusive law for the rehabilitation of those who are displaced from their homes and lands by these projects. Though lakhs of people have been displaced for ushering in development in independent India, by the state itself, there was no law or even a National Policy for their rehabilitation till now for about 60 years. Some state governments as well as some public sector companies have their own rehabilitation and resettlement policies. This Bill sought to provide the minimum basic requirements that all projects leading to involuntary displacement must address. The Bill was formulated in line with the National Rehabilitation and Resettlement Policy that became operative from October 31, 2007. During the same period, amendment to the Land Acquisition Act too was contemplated. It was then decided to merge these two components—land acquisition and R & R. The result was the Right to Fair Compensation and Transparency in Land Acquisition, Rehabilitation and Resettlement Act, 2013 (see Sec. 4.2 above for further details).

6

Land After Mining

There are no serious efforts to replace the lost flora or reclaim the land in the small iron ore/manganese mines in Noamundi block after mining is over. The mine owners plant some shrubs or trees which have no use value at all. Back-filling of rocks is not done normally. The rocks which cannot be used remain in heaps near the mine site itself and the topsoil is neither preserved nor replaced.

Some restoration of land is being undertaken in the big iron ore mines in and near Noamundi. The TISCO mine at Noamundi established a botanical garden and nursery at the reclaimed mine site. Similarly CCL has a model site at Piparwar where land was reclaimed after mining. However these are maintained by the companies as show-pieces to demonstrate their social responsibility and environmental consciousness; none of them follow the same practices of land reclamation at all their mine sites.

6.1 Giridih Experience: Continuing Impact of Mining and Displacement

Mining has continued in the colliery belt of Giridih for the last 100 years or more. First it was the Eastern Railway who was extracting coal from this region. Then the National Coal Development Corporation started mining operations in 1956. After nationalization and the formation of Coal India and its subsidiaries in 1973, CCL took over mining operations in this region. Today, there are hundreds of closed or abandoned mines all over the colliery belt extending from West Bengal to Jharkhand after more than a century of mining in this region. On the surface, these are just small holes; but they extend deep down into the earth's bosom. A person new to the area can easily fall into one of these holes and never come out. Animals can also disappear into these holes. There are many places in the colliery belt where, if you walk over the surface, you feel like you are walking over an empty shell and the earth can cave in any minute. Such accidents like that have actually happened. The recent accident in Jharia where some houses along with their inhabitants disappeared into a crater that developed on the earth surface must still be fresh in public memory.

None of the lands have been reclaimed or made suitable for cultivation in this area. The land is uneven, and the topsoil is destroyed. But even if the land were cultivable, it would have been of no use to the people as the land remains in the hands of the company even after the completion of mining. There is no law today that stipulates that land after mining should be returned to the original owners.

There are two rehabilitation sites of the Giridih Open Cast Project, namely, Prem Nagar and Gandhi Nagar. All the people who have been resettled in these colonies are Dalits, who lived in nearby villages for generations. They lost their lands and livelihoods to the mines and slowly became dependent on mining as the source of livelihood. But when the mines closed down, they lost this source of livelihood too. None of them have any land to cultivate or live on. There are no forests left in this region because of intensive mining. Left with no other option, they started going into the abandoned mines to extract whatever coal was left inside at great risk to their lives. Soon, middlemen appeared on the scene, offering some minimum equipment for extraction like shovels and buckets, and the agreement was, the extracted coal would be divided equally with them.

6.2 Illegal Coal Miners

Today, all the displaced families living in the rehabilitation sites, with the exception of those who got jobs in CCL, are engaged in 'illegal' cutting and selling of coal. They go into the holes left open in the abandoned coal mines of CCL and extricate the remaining coal and bring it out. Buyers wait outside with their cycles. Half the extracted coal goes to the contractor. The other half belongs to the miners, which they would either sell directly to the peddlers waiting outside or take it home and burn it into coke and sell at a higher price. The coal is taken over long distances by a relay of peddlers carrying the heavy loads on cycles. The fuel needs of the poor and middle class people in this region are met by this 'illegal' coal supply.

There are about 30,000 people in Giridih district alone who make their livelihood from this trade. They are into this extremely dangerous and taxing job because of the absence of any other options. Women and children also work in these 'illegal' mines. Economically this may be somewhat more profitable than other kinds of labour, but the dangers involved are tremendous. Within the crevasses of the underground mines the contractors, police agents, etc. molest and rape women and children. Those who go into the craters to cut coal work under very precarious conditions; there is the ever-present danger of mine-collapse. There are several hundreds of deaths each year with collapse of mine roofs. Many who are working in these illegal mines now are those who have lost their relatives in such mine accidents earlier, which shows the extent of their desparation. If there is a mine collapse, nobody dares to talk about it or try and retrieve the bodies of their relatives who died inside, for fear that the 'administration' would seal the mine and their '*choolas*' will not burn for days.

There is a strong 'contractor' mafia involved in this trade and making huge profits who has links with the revenue and police departments and CCL bureaucracy. The contractors pay them regularly to ensure that they turn a blind eye to what is happening. Where the payment is delayed, bulldozers come immediately, and raze the entrance to the mine.

7

Current Situation of Labour in Mines

The Mines Act 1952 regulates the working conditions, health and safety of workers working in all mines of major minerals. The Act very clearly spells out the minimum facilities that the mine owner or his representative has to provide to his employees working in such mines.

1. Drinking water, specially marked on the outside
2. Latrines and urinals, separately for men and women, maintained in a sanitary condition
3. Pit head baths in underground mines
4. First aid boxes and cupboards accessible at all times (in mines where there are more than 150 workers, there should be a room of the prescribed size)

In a study carried out in Chandil block in July 2003 among workers in stone quarries and crushers, it was found that none of these facilities were available to workers. Nor do they get benefits of welfare laws such as crèche, maternity leave with pay, medical facilities, leave facilities, medical insurance, etc. They do not have Provident Fund schemes either.

Similarly, in another study carried out in Noamundi block in 5 iron ore/manganese mines in December 2002, it was found that no facilities were provided to the workers as per the provisions of the Act, except for drinking water. Workers did not get a weekly paid holiday as stipulated in the Mining Act. There were no leave or medical facilities available to workers. There was no Provident Fund. The employers used various strategies to see that they escaped the obligation of paying Provident Fund to workers by giving them work for less than 20 days a month, entering false names in the roster and making workers discontinue after working for 11 months continuously. There is a hospital at Jamda near Noamundi built under the Cess Act for workers of small mines. This was inaugurated in 1978 with all the latest equipment, but sadly very few workers get treated there; there is only a skeletal staff there to run the hospital. Workers do not even know of the existence of such a health facility for them.

7.1 Working Hours and Wages

The Mining Act says that no adult working underground or overground shall work for more than 48 hours or 6 days per week. No person working overground shall work for more than 9 hours per day and no person working underground shall work for more than 8 hours per day at a stretch. If a person works longer than this, he/she should be paid twice the normal wages as overtime wages.

In Chandil region in Singhbhum East district, it was found that about 5,000 workers were working in stone quarries in 2003. All of them were temporary or casual labourers though they might have been working in these same mines for several years. They do not have access to the most basic facilities, nor do they enjoy basic rights. There are no overtime wages paid to any worker. They work on a piece rate basis. If they can fill a box with a volume of 100 cft, they get Rs. 80-100.[11] A person would take a minimum of two days to fill a box of that size. So a worker's daily earnings come to much less than the minimum wages announced by the state (which was Rs. 64 in 2003). The amount of labour required is also dependent on the location of the stone. If the

11. The current daily wages for unskilled labourers in the region is about Rs. 150 per day.

stone is on the top, then less work is involved. If it is deep below, then more time and work is required to take it first to the surface and then cut it. Since work is done on a piece-rate basis, there is no bar on the number of hours of work; the workers work for as long as they can.

In Noamundi, wages were paid on a piece-rate basis only in two of the mines. In one mine, each worker would earn about Rs. 38 per day by filling a box. In the other mine, the workers were getting Rs. 40 per day. In the rest, it was daily wages; but these also varied from mine to mine. In one mine Rs. 300 was paid to both male and female workers. In another, Rs. 50 was paid to men and Rs. 40 to women. In the third mine, Rs. 50 was paid to both men and women alike.

7.2 Child Workers

The Mines Act says that no child below the age of 18 shall be allowed to work in a mine. In the stone mines, most of the workers work as family units; as a result children are also involved in the work. It is found that there are even children from the age of 11 or 12 working in these mines.

In the small iron and manganese mines near Noamundi, in a study carried out in 2002, it was found that at least 30% of the workers were below the age of 18. This number has gone up in the last 5 years, as there was a phenomenal increase in the number of stone crushers and mines in this area. In Maralgada village close to Noamundi town, more than 25 crushers were working. All of them were started during the boom years in the last decade. A similar situation exists in most other villages surrounding Noamundi town. These crushers receive iron ore from small mines operating illegally, either inside the forest or on private lands, and therefore, the ore reaches the crushers at night. The workers in these small mines as well as crushers are mostly girls and boys below the age of 18. These young girls also work at night loading and unloading iron ore. Many of them may even be sexually exploited.

7.3 Sexual Exploitation of Women Workers

The Mines Act says specifically that women shall not be employed in any part of a mine which is underground. This rule is followed in the big mines; very few women are employed in these mines. But in the 'illegal' coal mines, women also go into the dark holes along with men to extract coal. The Act further specifies that women can be employed overground only between 6 am to 7 pm, a provision to protect women from sexual exploitation. In a study done in the Chandil area, it was found that there were two shifts daily in the stone crushers. 90% of the workers were women; so women are also employed in night shifts. It was reported that sexual exploitation of women workers by contractors, truck-drivers, or supervisors, who were often non-tribals and outsiders, was very common in these crushers. Many women give in for fear of losing their jobs or are forced into situations from where they cannot escape. The study showed that there were about 5-6 unmarried mothers among the women workers. It was also reported that many women workers approached private doctors in Chandil for medical termination of pregnancy. 99% of the women workers in the study area were Adivasis as other caste women do not go out for work in this area which is more Sanskritized than some other areas.

These issues of public health, occupational health, accidents and sexual exploitation of women workers are seldom addressed or recognized by the government or the concerned departments or even the public. There are some laws to address these, but law enforcing mechanisms that are supposed to check or control these problems are totally non-functioning.

7.4 Occupational Health of Mine Workers

Section 25 of the Mines Act says that if a worker contracts a disease notified in the Official Gazette as a disease connected with mining operations, the owner or manger of the mine has to send a notice to the Chief Mines Inspector and other authorities in such a form within such a period as may be prescribed. If a medical practitioner attends on a person who is/has been employed in a mine and who is believed by the medical practitioner to be suffering from any of the notified diseases, the medical practitioner shall, without delay, send a report in writing to the Chief Inspector of Mines stating the details of the patient, disease and the mine where he/ she was last employed in. If any practitioner fails to do that, he/she shall be punishable with a fine of Rs. 50. This has been amended to either three months' imprisonment or a fine of Rs. 1000.

The diseases that have been notified by the central government as diseases connected with mining operations so far are asbestosis, silicosis, coal workers' pneumoconiosis, cancer of the lungs (among uranium and asbestos miners), cancer of the peritoneum (uranium and asbestos) and manganese poisoning. The workers who are diagnosed to have contracted any of these diseases are entitled to compensation as per the Workmen's Compensation Act 1923.

7.5 Accidents in Stone Mines

Work in stone mines or stone crushers is hazardous, as chances of accidents are quite high.Pieces can go into the eyes of the workers and damage them while breaking stones. No safety gear is provided to workers in the stone crushers in the Chandil belt. Many fatal accidents happen in which workers get buried under rock or soil. If an accident happens causing injury to a person, the contractor gives first aid and forgets about it. In a more serious accident, the worker is taken to the hospital and then forgotten. The contractor does not give any compensation whatsoever, even when the injury causes disability nor does he pay for the treatment.

An Adivasi worker died in an accident in a stone mine at Chakulia village in Chandil block of Singhbhum East district. The contractor gave his family money for the funeral and got his body cremated as fast as possible without any medical examination or autopsy. The accident was not reported to any authority nor did anyone come to know of this incident. Any accident has to be reported by law and in case of fatal accidents, the Inspector of Mines should make an enquiry into the matter. The workers have no identification papers to show that they work in the mines. The contractors/ managers of these small mines and crushers do not keep a labour register or even if they do, they do not enter the correct names of workers.

7.6 Crusher Worker Dies of Silicosis

In February 2003, a man working in a stone crusher died of some illness which had the symptoms of silicosis in Teranga village, about 3 kms. from Ghatshila in Singhbhum East district. When a fact finding team visited the village on March 3, 2003, it was found that there were seven or eight other crusher workers from the same village who were also sick and suffering from similar symptoms. The team met an Adivasi doctor working at a private nursing home in Ghatshila who had attended to the patient a few days before his death. The doctor confirmed that the worker had been suffering from silicosis and said he was ready to testify in a court too if that was necessary. But another doctor in the same hospital, who was a non-Adivasi, was hostile and did not want to talk about the incident. He warned the Adivasi doctor not to talk as he was afraid he would be fined or taken to court. There are no medical facilities available to the workers working in these small mines or crushers, which abound in the whole of Singhbhum region and there is absolutely no recognition or onus on the employers for occupational diseases like silicosis.

8

Mining and its Impact on Health

The only functioning uranium mines in India are located at Jadugoda in East Singhbhum district. There are six uranium mines in the area now, including an open cast mine. A health study was carried out by Jharkhandis Organisation Against Radiation (JOAR) in 10 villages surrounding the Jadugoda mine in 1996. The survey showed a high incidence of a) congenital abnormalities or diseases, b) spontaneous abortions, c) neo-natal deaths, d) skin diseases including skin cancers, and e) lethargy/depression, among the nearly 10,000 population that was studied.

JOAR confronted the Uranium Corporation of India Limited (UCIL) management several times on the issue of radiation hazards on health; but the management did not acknowledge even once that there can be health hazards due to radiation. Whereas it is an internationally acknowledged fact that there are certain illnesses and congenital abnormalities or diseases caused by exposure to radiation. Continued exposure to low dose radiation can cause cancers, congenital problems like Down's Syndrome, etc. Studies all over the world have shown that uranium miners suffer from a high incidence of silicosis and lung cancers. But the scientists of the Bhabha Atomic Research Centre and other highly placed scientific institutions of this country fail to acknowledge these as possible consequences of radiation. Their constant refrain was and still is that if tribals are sick, it is because they have unhygienic habits and they drink. If their babies die, it is because of malnutrition.

The activists of JOAR point out the unwillingness on the part of the Atomic Energy Establishment to acknowledge the possibility of radiation-related illnesses in a population that is exposed to radiation in very many ways. Secondly, there is criminal negligence on the part of UCIL to protect and safeguard the health of their workers and families as well as the general population living in the vicinity. It flouts many national and international regulations for the safety of workers and villagers.

The underground mine workers are not provided with any safety gear except for helmets and gloves. But international experts say there is no equipment or gear that can provide protection from radiation. The workers have to undergo routine medical examinations once in six months. But the results of these tests are not revealed to them. The authorities say they cannot divulge the findings because these are official secrets and come under the Official Secrets Act. Many workers have chronic illnesses, but the doctors do not give them the correct diagnosis of their diseases. JOAR activists say that mortality rates among workers are very high.

International law requires that there should not be any habitation within 4 kms. radius of the mine. There is a village about half a km away from the tailing pond where the radioactive mine waste is dumped. But the regulation stipulates that this waste should always be kept below 2ft. of water, which is not followed in Jadugoda. The waste is mixed with water before it gets pumped into the tailing pond, but it soon dries up. In summer months a fine dust rises and travels into all the neighbouring villages, carried by wind. The waste water from the uranium milling plant flows into the river Subarnarekha. Authorities say it is treated water and there is no danger. But the local activists do not quite believe this. The rock waste from the uranium mine is used to build roads in the area and also in house construction.

A study was carried out in September 2002 by a team of doctors and epidemiologists brought together by Anumukti, an NGO from Gujarat, in 6 villages surrounding Jadugoda. They also conducted control studies in two other similar tribal areas. They found a significantly higher number of deformed people in the study area born after the start of mining operations. The number of children born with deformities in Jadugoda was found to be much higher than in the control area. Another important finding of the study was that there was an anomalously high incidence of tuberculosis (TB) or rather, chronic lung problems among uranium workers in the study area. Their conclusion was, some of these persistent TB cases could be that of lung cancer or silicosis.

A dossimetric study carried out by a scientist from Greenpeace International in September 2000 showed high levels of ambient radiation even on the roads, in and around houses and school buildings in Jadugoda area. The highest reading was on the railway platform from where uranium ore is transported to Hyderabad and the radioactive waste is unloaded which comes from Hyderabad to be disposed of in Jadugoda. The radon measurements were high inside some of the houses built with stones taken from the mine waste, higher than the limits prescribed by the Atomic Energy Regulatory Board.

8.1 Damodar: A River Killed by Mining

Damodar is a small rainfed river originating from the Khamerpet hill near the trijunction of Palamau, Hazaribagh and Ranchi districts. It flows through the cities of Ramgarh, Dhanbad, Asansol, Durgapur, Burdwan and Howrah, before joining the lower Ganga (Hoogly estuary) at Shayampur, 55 kms. downstream of Howrah. The river is fed by a number of tributaries at various reaches, the principal ones being Jamunia, Bokaro, Konar, Saifi, Bhera, Nalkari and Barakar. Today, this river, considered a sacred river by the local people, looks like a sewage canal, shrunken and filled with filth and rubbish, emanating obnoxious odours.

Damodar basin is the repository of nearly 46% of the coal reserves of India. Seven coalfields are presently located along this river. Because of the easy availability of coal in this belt, many coal-based industries like coal washeries, coke oven plants, coal fired thermal power plants and steel plants are also located along this river. The huge quantities of untreated industrial waste water that are discharged by these industries into the river, often containing toxic metals, are the main source of contamination of the river.

Mine water and run off through overburden material of the opencast mines also contribute towards the pollution of the river and other nearby water sources as well. Massive dumps of overburden material have been thrown on the banks of the river and its tributaries, which get carried into the river during rainy season. The large-scale mining operations going on in this area have adversely affected the ground water table in this area, with the result that the yield of water from rivers has drastically reduced. The effluents discharged from the mine site have seriously polluted the underground water of the area.

A study showed that heavy metals like manganese, chromium, lead, arsenic, mercury, cadmium and copper are found in the sediments and water of Damodar river and its tributaries like Safi river. The study warned that long-term exposure to lead present in the area might result in general weakness, anorexia, dyspepsia, metallic taste in the mouth, headache, drowsiness, high blood pressure, anaemia, etc.

The sediments are deficient in calcium and magnesium, but are rich in potassium. Titanium and iron are the dominant heavy metals found in the sediments. Silica content is high with a value of 28 ppm. Arsenic in the water ranges from 0.001 to 0.06 mg/l, mercury ranges from 0.0002 to 0.004 mg/l, and fluoride ranges from 1 to 3 mg/l. Strontium is found almost uniformly along the river bed, its concentration in the sediments being 130 ppm.

It is obvious that water resources have been badly contaminated due to extensive coal mining and vigorous growth of industries in the area. The people living in this area are forced to use this contaminated water as there is no alternate source of drinking water. Therefore, a sizeable part of the population suffers from water-borne diseases. A health survey of about three lakh population showed the most common diseases in this area as diarrhoea, dysentery, skin infections, worm infections, jaundice and typhoid. Dysentery and skin infections are exceptionally high.

8.2 Health Situation in East Parej Mine Area

In East Parej, more than 80% of the community lives in poverty. Water for the community comes from hand pumps, dug wells, local streams and rivers. Dug wells dry up in summer and even in winter. For the villagers of Agaria *tola*, their only source of drinking water has been damaged due to dumping of overburden and expansion of opencast mine. Water from the hand pumps of the area often has a foul smell and taste. They have to walk an average of 1-2 kms to get safe drinking water, which distance increases in summer months. As a result, people are forced to drink the contaminated water.

'Our longevity has reduced drastically', says Phulmoni Kujur, a 38-year-old woman of East Parej. Mahesh, a Santhal from the same village, said that the villagers bathe only after 5 to 10 days, and do not drink water adequately due to water pollution. The study reveals that the average longevity of women in East Parej coalfield area was 45 years and in most villages only one or two women had crossed the age of 60. In North Karanpura Coal field area, the average longevity of males is 50 years and that of females is 45 years.

The number of deaths in a period of five years in East Parej are shocking: Dudhmatia village – 6 out of 80 people; Agaria *tola* – 12 out of 100 people; Lopangtandi –13 out of 115 people; and Ulhara – 9 (7 of these children) out of 80 people.

The majority of the population in North Karanpura Coalfields area is dependent on the Safi river for drinking and other domestic purposes. The river is highly polluted because of the presence of coalmines waste dumped along the banks of the river at many locations. The water contains toxic metals like arsenic and mercury. Manganese has crossed the maximum permissible toxic levels (3.6 mg/l against the permissible level of 0.5 mg/l.) According to WHO, high manganese levels can cause lethargy, increased muscle tone and mental disturbances. A health survey done among the boys and girls in a local school showed that most of the children (both tribal and non-tribal) are lethargic, probably due to the inhalation of coal dust and consumption of water with high manganese levels.

Malaria is a very common killer disease in these mining areas. There are numerous ditches in the mining site and open tanks which breed mosquitoes. Most of the deaths in the area were attributed to malaria. Many, especially children, suffer from dysentery and diarrhoea and die. About 60% of the people are affected by seasonal allergies. Skin diseases like eczema are highly prevalent in this area. High nickel content in water (0.024 mg/l has been reported in some areas) could be one of the causes. Nickel is a common skin allergen. TB, headache, joint pain (pain begins at the age of 5 to 10 years in North Karanpura region), gastric diseases, cold and cough and asthma are the other reported illnesses. The people are more dependent on quacks for healthcare needs in the absence of any functioning government medical facilities in these places. There is a hospital run by Central Coalfields Limited, but it is only for their employees.

8.3 Roro Asbestos Mines

Hyderabad Asbestos Company, a subsidiary of Birlas, was operating an asbestos mine at Roroburu near Chaibasa in Singhbhum West district, which they closed down around 30 years ago. About 2,500 workers worked in the mine at the time of closure. Newspapers reported that before the closure, many of the workers suffered from asbestosis, a fatal disease, which the company refused to acknowledge. In 1982, they closed down the mines summarily, stopped all operations and left without any notice to the workers. Those workers who were ill were deprived of any compensation or healthcare support. Many did not even receive their last months' wages. It was rumoured that the company abandoned the mines to avoid paying any damages to their workers who were suffering from serious mine-related illnesses. Besides, they also left behind huge quantities of hazardous chemical waste without providing any mechanisms to store or dispose of the waste safely or prevent it from entering and polluting air and water in the area.

A Fact Finding Team (FFT) set up by Mines, Minerals and People (MM & P), a national alliance of mining affected communities and Bindrai Institute for Research, Study and Action (BIRSA), Chaibasa visited the abandoned mine site in December 2002. The team noted that the dumpsites where the mine waste had been dumped could pose a serious threat to the health of the people living in the villages below. The mine was located on a hill with the maximum elevation being 600 m below which the villages of Tilaisud and Roro are situated. The biggest dumpsite faces the Roro village directly, which can be sighted from a few kilometres from the road below. The waste dumped at this particular site at the highest point spreads across 100 m. All the dumpsites can potentially contaminate the streams flowing down the hills and ponds located in the village with suspended and dissolved material. The stream carries the particles probably several kilometres downstream. The naturally occurring chromites can contaminate the water in the form of hexavalent chromium and nickel.

The FFT in its report notes that 'the dumpsites pose proximate exposure to children and elderly, who tend cattle crossing this route to graze animals at higher parts of the hill which are thickly forested. Also of graver concern is the fact that the relatively soft waste material over the slope is a matter of entertainment for the children who slide down the slope raising dusty clouds of lethal wastes. Asbestos with chromite and nickel dust is hardly 300 m. about to reach the River Roro to contaminate the river water directly. Bad days await the local tribal people after two or three monsoons if precautions are not taken.' These words were written over a decade ago, but hardly any precautions have been taken by the authorities till now! This is not surprising, as it is the normal practice followed in all operational and abandoned mines, not to bother about cleaning up the surroundings after mining is done. But in this case, it is lethal wastes that are strewn around.[12]

Mines Concession Rules lays down detailed procedures for the protection of environment, prevention of pollution and destruction to environment, buildings, structures and restoration of lost flora, to be followed in all mining operations. It details how the overburden, waste rock and fines should be kept in separate dumps and secured so that they do not escape into the environment. It also insists on back-filling of these wastes into the mine excavations, after mining operations are concluded with a view to restore the land to its original use as far as possible. And where back-filling is not possible, the waste dumps shall be suitably terraced and stabilised through vegetation or otherwise. It adds that the fines, rejects or tailings from mine, beneficiation or metallurgical plants shall be deposited and disposed in a specially prepared tailings disposal area such that they are not allowed to flow away from and cause land degradation and damage to agricultural land, pollution of surface water bodies and ground water or cause floods.

8.4 Water/Air Pollution

The Tata Steel Limited (formerly Tata Iron and Steel Company Limited—TISCO) has polluted the surface and underground water in Noamundi. They have built dams for

---

12. A petition was filed in January 2014 in the National Green Tribunal at Delhi seeking a judicial order to clear the hazardous wastes from the dumpsite at Roroburu.

carrying water from washeries and workshops; this water is purified and sent to the streams. During the rainy season, reddish water from the dams escape into the tiny rivulet flowing close by, which is the main water source for many villages nearby. The sewage from the TISCO colony is also emptied into the river system. The contaminated water causes skin diseases and gastro-intestinal diseases in the population around. The red water that escapes into the nearby agricultural fields destroys the crops and the fertility of the soil. The underground water in this area is highly polluted with a high content of iron and other chemicals.

9

Resistance in the New Period

There have been many struggles against mining companies in Jharkhand; some were spontaneous struggles while others were organised and well-planned. How many of these struggles succeeded in achieving their goals? It is hard to say.

The efforts of the state and central governments to prioritise mining as the key industry in Jharkhand and accelerate the industrialisation of Jharkhand by inviting private companies to invest in mining has met with stiff resistance in some areas. When the Jharkhand government went on a signing spree with various mining companies from both outside and inside the state in 2005, ten different organizations working in Singhbhum district got together and formed a coordination under the banner of the Mucha committee (meaning umbrella) and they toured the whole of Singhbhum West district organizing village meetings and informing people of the impending threat to their lands due to mining. Singhbhum, because of its rich reserves of iron ore and manganese, has attracted the attention of many investing companies. According to newspaper reports, by early 2005, the Jharkhand government had signed 43 MOUs with different companies, most of which were in Singhbhum district.

9.1 Fight Against the Essar Company

In 2004, news appeared in local newspapers that the Essar Company wanted to start a steel plant at Purana Manoharpur, in Manoharpur block of Singhbhum West district. They were planning to acquire 3,000 acres of land displacing 7 villages. Most of the lands were very good agricultural lands belonging to private individuals, and the rest were village common lands. No forest land was involved though these villages are all very close to the forest. When the news came, village meetings were held in all the villages by the Gram Ganraj Block Committee and JOHAR (Jharkhandis Organisation for Human Rights) The meetings helped to create an awareness and knowledge among villagers of what were the future prospects for them. Village elders and informed persons from the community like teachers, ex-army men, social activists and others attended these meetings regularly. A coordination committee was formed with traditional heads and representatives from all the seven villages which were expected to be displaced. Public opinion was very strong. They did not want to give up their lands. The villagers then came to know that Tata Steel and Dempo Goa were also interested in acquiring land for setting up steel plants in Manoharpur block. This further ignited public resentment and strengthened the resistance. Thousands of people from Manoharpur area participated in the rally that was held at Chaibasa on November 10, 2005.

Essar had appointed Jayant Jaipal Singh, the son of the legendary Jharkhandi leader and politician, Jaipal Singh, as one of their senior officers and sent him to Manoharpur to influence the villagers in the company's favour. Jaipal Singh hailed from the *Munda* community and Manoharpur is an area with a large *Munda* population. Jayant Jaipal Singh had meetings with some members of the coordination committee and he managed to influence the chairperson of the committee, Basant Naik, in favour of the company. The committee decided to have a large procession on November 17 and submit a memorandum to the Circle Officer (CO), stating their decision not to give land to the company. Basant Naik who was entrusted with the responsibility to draft the memorandum, wrote that the people were willing to give up their lands on condition that the company provided jobs for each family, school, hospital and other facilities. When the procession set out, Basant Naik and some of his supporters remained in the front and manipulated things in such a way that by the time the other leaders and people came to the CO's office, this Memorandum was already submitted to the CO without the approval of the people's assembly.

In the meeting ground when the agenda for the meeting was finalising the Memorandum and submitting it to the CO was taken up, the Chairman of the committee told the assembly that the memorandum was already submitted and also received by the CO. This surprised and angered the people and they asked him to get it back from the CO immediately. The Memorandum was then read out publicly. People were shocked and infuriated to see the content that was exactly opposite to what they had decided earlier. They demanded that the Memorandum be torn up in front of the assembly and the coordination committee was disbanded with immediate effect. Jayant Jaipal Singh had to withdraw from the scene after this incident, and subsequently, Essar Company withdrew their decision to start the steel plant in Manoharpur.

Essar then came to Ulijhari near Chaibasa in Sadar block. They contacted Antu Hembrom, the head of the Munda Manki Sangh, the organisation of traditional village heads. Through him, they started convincing villagers and organizing medical camps in the villages. Jayant Jaipal Singh was seen meeting him once or twice. The villagers realized that Antu was playing the role of middleman for the company. They caught him, beat him up, paraded him with *chappal malas* (garlands of footwear) in the marketplace and surrendered him to the police and lodged an FIR against him for cheating.

9.2 Fighting Tatas

At Gudusai near Chakradharpur where the Tata Company wanted to set up a plant, the company officers had come to measure the land accompanied by some policemen. Some villagers, including women, who were there on the site at the time protested asking them why they had come. Police started beating them up. The whole village came out in defence and beat up the policemen. The company people did not dare to return again to that village.

In another incident in Manoharpur block in Hakugui village, Tata Steel wanted to set up their plant. Some of their officers, along with the *amin*, came directly to the village one day and started measuring land. Some women saw these people and they pressed the alarm bell. The whole village assembled; the Tata Steel people confronted them with statements that they were against development. The infuriated village women beat up the company people. The *amin* went and filed an FIR against the village men alleging that they were preventing him from carrying out his duty. A case of criminal assault was also filed against three persons named in the FIR. This further angered the people. They hold regular village meetings and have resolved not to give their agricultural lands to the company at any cost.

Unfortunately, some villagers belonging to the Mahato[13] community had already given their lands to Dempo Goa in return for cash compensation. This created a division in the area. Tata company tried to get land in the villages of Badupos, Ghaghra, Raidih, Jojoghuttu and Mahuldiah. They contacted villagers and took the youth to Jamshedpur where they were given vocational trainings by Tata Steel Welfare Society. Health camps were also held. These villages were predominantly Mahato villages. There are not many Adivasi villages in this list. In Raidih, Jojoghuttu and Mahuldiah,

---

13. A politically powerful local community, who are non-Adivasis.

which are pure Adivasi villages, people have warned the Mahatos that if they gave their lands to the company, they would not be allowed to enter the forests.

In Dimbuli, Kamarbeda and Dautumba villages, Dempo Goa started taking land from Mahato families. There were some families having land in two different places. First they had acquired 3 acres of land. After talking to all the neighbouring villagers, belonging to Mundari, Mahato and Nayak families, the company acquired about 300 acres of land. Dempo also organised medical camps and distributed footballs, jerseys and blankets, and offered money for organising pujas, tournaments, medical treatment, meeting marriage expenses, etc. Besides, they also appointed 12 young men to persuade the villagers to give their lands. The company signed an agreement with 32 *raiyats*. Despite the resistance of the majority of the villagers, the company managed to recruit some to their side and take land.

9.3 Struggle in North Karanpura Valley: Public Hearings as a Weapon

North Karanpura valley on Upper Damodar is one of the largest coal-bearing belts in the Jharkhand region. It is also a very important heritage site with its ancient rock caves and rock paintings dating back to the Paleolithic period. This heritage site is facing threats of imminent destruction because of the proposed coal mines in the valley. Two very large open cast mines planned by CCL, Magadh and Amrapali are in the Karanpura valley. The National Thermal Power Coporation (NTPC) wants to set up a thermal power plant and a mine to supply the necessary coal for the thermal plant in the valley. Besides, there are many other smaller mines which are being planned in this belt.

NTPC had chosen its site in Barkagaon block of Hazaribagh district. Twenty-six villages would be totally displaced by the project. Most of the people living in these villages are Dalits who had been brought from Gaya generations ago by the zamindars to work for them. They had worked as bonded labourers for generations and finally they won their freedom from the zamindars after a long struggle in the 1990s. This created in them awareness and a zeal to fight for their rights. Many Dalit families had bought small plots of land in the Karanpura area with their hard-earned money. EMTA, Nico-Jaiswal and Abhijeet groups are also eyeing this area for their mining activities; together they will displace another 12 villages. On the whole, 38 villages have been targeted for displacement in this block.

It is mandatory for any big project of more than 25 hectares to hold an Environmental Public Hearing, where a report of assessment of the proposed project will be presented before the public. Advance information about the Public Hearing has to be given to the public through newspapers. Villagers from the surrounding villages as well as NGOs and concerned individuals can attend these Public Hearings and give their views on the project's environmental impact and ask for clarifications from the lessee. An environmental clearance is a necessary pre-condition for any major project as per law. In the Karanpura valley, people have continually rejected Public Hearings, and did not allow them to take place. They have demonstrated through this their resolve not to give any land for mining, not even an inch. EMTA had announced an Environmental Public Hearing for their project in 2005 to be held at Badam village in Barkagaon block, one of the affected villages. Nearly 7,000 women and men, carrying the banner of Karanpura Bachao Sangharsh Samiti, went and sat on the dais. They did not allow the officers from EMTA or the State Pollution Control Board (SPCB) to even approach the dais.

A second Public Hearing was organised jointly by EMTA and Nico-Jaiswal at the same venue, but it had to be postponed due to public protest. A third Public Hearing was organised jointly by the same companies at Hazaribagh, the district headquarters, as they feared a similar fate this time too. They thought if they shifted the venue to a distant place, villagers would not be able to come. But contrary to their expectations, people arrived in large numbers; there was a massive protest and the public gheraoed the DC's office.

Following this, another Public Hearing was announced by NTPC on January 6, 2007 at 11 am. But fearing public protest, the Public Hearing was held secretly from 11 pm the previous night at the District Control Room Hall at Hazaribagh in the presence of the District Pollution Control Board members, NTPC officers, police and journalists, along with some community members who had been bought over by the company. When the villagers got news of the Public Hearing being held surreptiously, about 100-150 of them rushed to the venue and stopped the hearing. This was followed by some pushing, shoving and angry scenes. The district administration declared Section 144 in the area, prohibiting all meetings and gatherings. Defying this, the villagers took out a protest rally in the town the next day which blocked the road traffic completely. The SDO was forced to come for talks; he promised the people that police cases would not be filed against any of them. But later, violating this agreement, cases were filed against 24 villagers and two persons were arrested. Deepak Das and Rafeeq Ansari spent 65 and 63 days respectively in jail. NTPC had built an office in Barkagaon, the inauguration of which was supposed to be held in November 2006. Villagers had assembled on the premises on that day and in a show of anger and dismissal, they broke chairs, tables, windows and doors of the new building. Criminal cases were filed against Loknath Mahato, the local MLA and 500 others for vandalizing the office. But the company agreed to drop these cases later during negotiation talks with the villagers.

On April 16, 2007, a second Public Hearing was called by NTPC at the Barkagaon block office. CRPF had been called in by the company for protection. The day before the Public Hearing, CRPF carried out a flag march in Barkagaon. On the day of the hearing, CRPF jawans were posted on all the main roads and junctions to dissuade people from attending. But despite all this, villagers, nearly 10,000 of them, assembled at the meeting grounds. The villagers demanded that a bigger *shamiana* be erected, so that all those who had come to attend the Public Hearing could sit under it. They then removed all chairs and tables and everybody sat down on the floor, including the SP, DSP, revenue officers and the SPCB members. They asked the local MLA, Loknath Mahato, who was present, on whose side he was, and asked him to sit with them if he was on their side. They demanded to get a report of what the company had done after the previous Public Hearing where they had voiced their concerns and views. They asked R.B. Pathak, the General Manager, why he was there, when they had made it clear that they did not want him to enter their villages again. They also demanded to know about the status of the criminal cases the company had promised to be withdrawn but nothing had happened. NTPC officials had no reply to all these questions. At the end, they told the people they would not attend another Public Hearing and left.

But subsequently, land acquisition proceedings were initiated in the area, and notifications issued through newspapers. The Circle Officer organised a camp for verification of land documents under the directions of the district administration. The people rejected this camp and sat on *dharna* in front of the block office for one week continuously. Finally, the Circle Officer had to close down the camp.[14]

9.4 Experience of Public Hearings in Noamundi

The Public Hearings which were held in the Saranda area in Singhbhum district give another side of the story. A total of nine Public Hearings were held here in the course of the three years. The first of such Public Hearings, was held for the

14. Due to the consistent and determined struggles of the people of Karanpura Valley under 'Karanpura Bachao Samiti' none of the 32 companies who had signed MOUs with the Jharkhand state government could start their plants in Jharkhand so far.

expansion of Tata Steel mines at Noamundi. The venue was the middle school inside the Tata Steel colony. The villagers did not know about the Public Hearing till activists of JOHAR, a human rights organisation, gave them the information. The villagers from 6 or 7 villages surrounding the mines, nearly 1500 men and women, went to attend the Public Hearing on the appointed day. Seeing them, Tata Steel authorities ordered the gates to be closed and the people were stopped from getting inside. This made the people angry and they blocked the traffic on the main road. The chairman of the Jharkhand State Pollution Control Board (JSPCB) came up to them asking some of their representatives to participate in the Public Hearing. The villagers refused and they lodged a complaint with the Chairman demanding him to announce the Public Hearing as illegal as the villagers had no prior information and those who wanted to attend the Public Hearing were physically prevented from attending it. But in spite of the strong protest of the people and the questions raised on the legality of the Hearing, the JSPCB gave environmental clearance to the project.

In a village called Bokna within the Saranda region in West Singhbhum district, the villagers came to know of the Public Hearing that was going to take place in their village from the activists of a women's organisation working in the area. The villagers attended the Public Hearing which was held at the village itself, and they expressed their strong protest and later wrote to the SPCB and the state government demanding the cancellation of the Public Hearing. But this project too got environmental clearance.

In another project located in the heart of Saranda, near Karampada, the activists of the women's organisation informed the heads of all the surrounding villages about the forthcoming Public Hearing and they all agreed that they would need to resist the coming of the mines as it would destroy the forest and impact their livelihoods. The Environment Public Hearing (EPH) was held at Kiriburu, about 30 kms away from the proposed site in the guest house of SAIL company. On the day of the Public Hearing, the village heads were seen sharing the dais with the officials of the company as well as the JSPCB and being garlanded by the company representatives. None of the other villagers were present on the occasion to give their views. Obviously, the company officials had done their homework and 'managed' to get the village *mundas* (traditional heads) onto their side, before the Public Hearing could take place. At Sasopi and Tankura, two other villages in Noamundi block, the Public Hearings were 'successful'.

At the Public Hearing in Khas Jamda, the company was afraid that there was going to be a protest from the villagers. So they used some new tactics to silence the dissenters by threatening them that they would be garlanded with *chappals* and paraded in the village. The company obviously could divide the village community and using the villagers who were on their side, pressurized the rest to keep quiet threatening them that if they opposed the mine, they would have to feed them and their families, as they did not have any other livelihood!

In Maralgada area, Public Hearings were held for two mines in June-July 2007. Rungta Company held an EPH at the Government High School at Noamundi for a mine they were operating for nearly two years. Two women from the nearby village spoke strongly against the mine in Ho language. When it was translated into Hindi, the tone of their speeches changed to being mild and compromising. At the second Public Hearing held for another mine in the forest near Maralgada and Duccasai villages, there was vehement opposition, especially from the women of these two villages, though there were some members from the community who supported the mine. The women strongly opposed the impact of the mine on their sacred place which fell within the lease area and also on the forest and environment. The villagers demanded that JSPCB members record the views of the women and cancel the lease on environmental grounds. They said they would look into the matter seriously and give their opinion later. But two weeks later, the company started fencing work on the proposed mine site!

Evidently the companies always tried to stage-manage Public Hearings. Initially, they used to bring people from distant villages, their employees and other supporters whom they could influence or buy over. Local villagers used to be absent from the scene. But of late, they seem to have given up on this tactic. They are investing more money and effort into buying local support from the affected villages themselves. They create divisions within the village into those who want mines and those who do not want mines. They give enticements to people in terms of money, two-wheelers for the village leaders, mobile phones for the educated young people, promise of jobs and other facilities. The companies enjoy the full support and backing of the State Pollution Control Board and the district administration. The present JSPCB chairman is singularly famous for his sympathies towards mining companies and the all-out support he gives them.[15]

15. This situation has changed in the last 5-6 years. A committee of villagers to protect their lands named 'Jameen Bachao Samanvatya Samiti'was formed and they have successfully resisted the entry of new mines and plants into the area. So far, they have stopped four companies from holding Public Hearings for setting up their plants within Noamundi block.

10

Conclusion

Mining is projected as the surest and perhaps the only way to economic and social development in Jharkhand today. In order to give strength to this argument, the attempt is to glorify the economic potential of mining in employment and income generation, development of ancillary industries, infrastructural development, etc. and conceal its destructive potential. Mining surely creates jobs, employment and increased cash inflow into the area. But what has been its impact on local, indigenous communities who lived in the area before mining began? How many of them have benefited from mining? What are the changes in their standards of living? What has been the impact of mining on the health of these communities living close to the mines? What about the impact of mining on forests, rivers, underground water, land, soil and wildlife? It is important to answer these questions honestly before opening the doors to more intensive and accelerated mining.

Displacement has far-reaching economic, social and cultural consequence on the lives of the people who are displaced, whether for hydro-electric power projects or mining and allied Industries. It starves people off from their traditional livelihoods, breaks up close-knit village communities and families, converts a self-reliant land-owning people into landless labourers and forces many to migrate to cities. The traditional value system based on equality and cooperation gets completely destroyed.

This has serious consequences on the life of the community and especially the women among them. Alcoholism becomes a way out and is found rampant among mining communities everywhere. Violence against women increases both within and outside homes. In addition, migration of non-Adivasi people to these mining sites leads to sexual harassment and exploitation of women. The incidence of sexually transmitted diseases like HIV tends to increase with the influx of outsiders. Malnutrition is common among women and children in the area.

In the colliery belt, evicted and cut-off from their traditional livelihoods, they are thrown into the mining towns where, if lucky, they get jobs as casual labourers. When the coal in the mine gets exhausted, they are once again thrown into an ever-expanding jobless market. Left with no food, they, together with their families, crawl into the abandoned mines and scavenge for the leftovers.

Scavenging has now become an industry in itself. Contractors, police, politicians, coal traders etc. all take their toll from the scavengers. With what is left, they load it on to bicycles and take it to the towns and cities for sale. They peddle it through perilous forest and steep mountain roads. The State and Industry call them illegal coal miners. There are over half a million of these bicycle coal peddlers in Jharkhand today. On every road of Jharkhand you see the open veins of what industrial development or national development has done to these first peoples.

The condition of workers in the unorganised sector, working in the small mines and crushers is very pitiable. The legal provisions for their welfare are not complied with in most of these mines. The wages paid are often less than the stipulated minimum wages. Women workers face sexual harassment and exploitation at the workplace. There are many single mothers living in the shanty towns adjoining mining areas. Child workers below the age of 18 constitute at least 30% of the workforce in the small mines and crushers.

Health hazards related to mining have not yet received

any serious attention as a major public health issue. The damaging effects of radiation on the health of miners and their families as well as the villagers living in surrounding villages of the uranium mine in Jadugoda is an issue that has been constantly pushed under the carpet by the company as well as the government. Safety regulations and norms are flouted with impunity, whether it is in Jadugoda or Roro or in any mine dealing with hazardous minerals and chemical substances. Occupational health of mine workers, especially in the unorganised sector is an area that is totally untouched.

Mining is responsible for a great deal of environmental pollution, which also goes unnoticed in the quest for 'development'. Rivers and streams are polluted and die off. Water level falls and even underground water gets polluted by the chemicals seeping in. River Damodar, which carries a major portion of the coal deposits of Jharkhand in its womb, is a living example to this. Dense, thick forests are cut down and invaluably rich bio-diversity lost forever. Air pollution causes innumerable health problems to villagers living nearby. Good, cultivable lands are destroyed without any hope for repair.

The social, cultural and environmental costs of mining should be taken into account, while working out the economics of mining. Similarly the health cost that communities and workers have to pay for mining. The governments should understand this and begin to fulfil their constitutional obligation to the people, especially the vulnerable and gullible Adivasis, of protecting their interests and not that of the big companies alone. The governments should also look at the massive environmental destruction that is happening all around in the quest for money and profit. If this is not curbed, the very existence of humans on this earth is at risk.

References

Anjum A. and A. Manthan. Review of the Rehabilitation Policy of Coal India in *Rehabilitation Policy and Law in India: A Right to Livelihood*, Fernandes, W. and Paranjpay, V. (eds) Indian Social Institute, Delhi and ECONET, Pune, 1997.

Bahl, Vinay. *The Rise and Growth of the Indian Steel Industry and its Workers' Struggle, 1880-1946,* Dissertation Submitted to the Graduate School of the University of New York, 1991.

Centre for Education & Communication. *Mining for Whom? A Dossier on Mines and Minerals*, New Delhi, 2000.

Department of Industries, Government of Jharkhand. *Industrial Policy of Jharkhand,* 2001.

Elwin, Verrier. *The Agaria,* Calcutta, 1942.

Ekka, Alexius and Asif Mohammed. *Development Induced Displacement and Rehabilitation in Jharkhand, 1951 to 1955: A Database on its Extent and Nature,* Indian Social Institute, New Delhi, 2000.

Fernandes, W. and V. Paranjpay (eds). *Rehabilitation Policy and Law in India: A Right to Livelihood,* Indian Social Institute, Delhi and ECONET, Pune, 1997.

Fernandes, Walter. *The Land Acquisition (Amendment) Bill 1998: For Liberalisation or for the Poor,* Indian Social Institute, New Delhi, 1999.

Frontline. Mining Better, 2008, pp.102-104.

Guha, R. and M. Gadgil. State Forestry and Social Conflict in British India in *Past and Present,* No. 123, 1989.

Justice Kumar, Gyanendra and Justice Malik, S. *D.D. Seth's Encyclopaedia of Mining Laws,* Delhi Law House, 1999.

Justice Shanmugham, K. *Law of Land Acquisition and Compensation*, Butterworths India, New Delhi, 2001.

Kumar, Sobhana Sadan. *Mining and the Raj*, Janaki Prakashan, Patna, 1996.

Management Report and Recommendation in Response to the Inspection Panel Investigation Report No. 24000, India: Coal Sector Environmental and Social Project (Credit No. 2862-IN), July 25, 2003.

Mines, Minerals and People, 2003. *National Seminar on Women and Mining in India: A Report*, Hyderabad.

Ministry of Mines & Geology, 2003. *Mineral Resources of Jharkhand*, Government of Jharkhand.

Nelson, John P. *Social Inequality and Political Structures*, Manohar Publications, New Delhi, 1983.

Pandey, R. and N. Roy. *Handbook of Chota Nagpur Tenancy Laws*, Rajpal & Company, Allahabad, 2002.

Prakash, Amit. *Jharkhand: Politics of Development and Identity*, Orient Longman, Hyderabad, 2001.

Pramanik, P. *Coal Miners in Private and Public Sector Collieries*, Reliance Publishing House, New Delhi, 1993.

Priyadarshi, Nitish. *Environmental and Health Impact Assessment Due to Coal Mining in East Parej and North Karanpura Coalfield of Jharkhand State, India: A Case Study.*

Rothermund D., E. Kropp, and G. Dienemann. *Urban Growth and Rural Stagnation*, Manohar Publications, New Delhi, 1980.

Rothermund, D. and D.C. Wadhwa. *Zamindars, Mines and Peasants*, Manohar Publications, New Delhi, 1978.

Samata. *Surviving a Mine Field: An Adivasi Triumph*, Hyderabad, 2003.

Sharma, B.D. *The Fifth Schedule (Vol. 1&2)*, Sahyog Pustak Kuteer Trust, New Delhi, 2000.

The Inspection Panel Investigation Report, India: Coal Sector Environmental and Social Mitigation Project (Credit No. 2862), November 25, 2002

Vagholikar, N. and K.A. Moghe. *Undermining India: A Report on Impacts of Mining on Ecologically Sensitive Areas in India*, Kalpavriksh, Pune, 2003.